I0119215

PRAISE FOR NOT CRAZY, JUST HUMAN

"**This is a book for all human kind.** This book confronts the emotional turmoil, silent suffering and negative self-talk experienced by family, friends and survivors of suicide. It further explores the journey of health and wellness, and the reality that the hard work is definitely worth it. As a fellow survivor of trauma, Deri's story and her willingness to share the depth of her lived experiences provided me with a deeper perspective of my own struggles. **The strength she demonstrates in the struggle is palpable** and the joy and love of connecting human kind is her gift."

Lieutenant-Colonel Trisha MacLeod, Commanding Officer, Canadian Forces Health Services (Canadian Armed Forces)

"Deri Latimer offers us a window into her experience with trauma, loss, and mental wellness. **Her vulnerability is so powerful and a wonderful example of healing and hope.** I am impressed with Deri's ability to tell her story with such openness. Anyone who has experienced grief, loss, shame, trauma, or mental health challenges will resonate with Deri's story in her book, Not Crazy, Just Human, as she shows us that it is okay to be vulnerable and ask for help and support."

Kelly Penner Hutton, Ph.D., C.Psych, Clinic Director, Peace of Mind Therapy and Consultation

"**A raw and authentic look at how sucking it up may sometimes suck you down.** It doesn't matter who you are, even an international speaker on positive emotion can experience overwhelming negative emotion. Deri shares her experience of being in the depths of despair and her slow climb out with pearls of wisdom for those of us who may be there or those of us who want to support a loved one who is there."

Mary Ann Baynton, MSW, Principal of Mary Ann Baynton & Associates, Director of Collaboration and Strategy for Workplace Strategies for Mental Health, and advisor to Mindful Employer Canada and My Workplace Health

"**Not Crazy, Just Human** *is a must read. While we all face adversity in our life, Deri's journey to wellness demonstrates how each of us has the capacity to transform trauma, stress and adversity into an opportunity for personal growth. The insights and authentic life lessons of this book make it a resource that you will want to keep on your shelf so that when you—or someone you know—are called upon to answer to a crisis, you will have Deri's wisdom to draw upon.* **This is an authentic and uplifting book** *that demonstrates why during life's darker moments we need to be our own best advocate, to always ask the hard questions, and to never give up until we get the right answers."*

Meg Soper, R.N., Motivational Humorist,
Co-Author of *From the Stage to the Page*

"**Raw, real and an empathy-stirring read** *is exactly what Deri provides to readers through her powerful journey of trauma to healing. Its page turning stories are captivating and illustrate why conversations around mental health aren't just important, but necessary."*

Codi Shewan, Speaker, Consultant, Author of
Everyday Legacy - Lessons For Living With Purpose, Right Now

"*This book is perfect for people who wonder why everyone else seems to have it all together and they don't. Every human being experiences shame, discomfort, and trauma in their lives. In this raw and authentic book, Deri shares what that looked like for her.* **She normalizes trauma and teaches us to face it with courage.** *Deri's very human journey is both inspiring and mobilizing!"*

Jennifer Kilimnik, Director, Culture & Compassion,
Rèseau Compassion Network

"*I invite readers to join Deri on the human journey by reading this book.* **It is very personal, yet I believe the most personal is also the most universal.** *Deri offers you a ride through the turbulent ocean of her experiences while providing you with a number of insights and lessons to assist you in building a raft to navigate through your own, absolutely human, life."*

David Zinger, JAH (Just Another Human), Author of *Zengage: How to Get More Into Your Work to Get More Out of Your Work*

"Not Crazy, Just Human *is a transparent and vulnerable portrayal of the author, who appeared to have it all but still could be paralyzed by trauma.* **It is a candid and self-reflective read that gives you permission to self-examine.** *As I was engrossed in the short story, I couldn't help forgive myself for not always having it together. I can now recognize that it is ok to feel crippled and overwhelmed, while not completely understanding the source.* **The story doesn't leave you in a pile of inadequacy. It empowers you** *by providing strategies to take action to find a way out of your circumstance (or trauma)."*

Suzanne F. Stevens, CSP, Concious-Contribution Cultivator, YouMeWe Social Impact Group Inc., Author of *Make Your Contribution Count for You, Me, We*

"*Deri has chronicled her journey to healing through a moving personal history. This book is a guiding light of hope for others who struggle to heal from past traumas. Her courage in sharing her story will inspire others to keep searching for the help they need.* **This book proves that even the most positive people can go through some dark times.** *Resilience is not about ignoring the circumstances; it's about fully processing the past."*

Anders Boulanger, Founder and CEO of Engagify

Deri Latimer's brave account of her personal journey allows the reader to explore topics such as mental health and recovery in a way that deepens understanding and provides insights and hope. **I wish I had her book while my brother was still alive, and I know I would have shared it with him.** *I believe her book would have benefited both of us in meaningful and diverse ways. I would recommend "Not Crazy Just Human" to anyone who is struggling with their own mental health or that of someone they love.*

Jennifer Spear, President and Creative Strategist, Clean Slate Strategies

NOT CRAZY,
Just Human

by

DERI LATIMER

A WOOD DRAGON BOOK

Not Crazy, Just Human -
Moving Through Trauma To Healing

All rights reserved. This book or any portion thereof
may not be reproduced in part or in whole without the
express written permission of the author except for the
use of brief quotations in a critical review.

Copyright 2021 Deri Latimer
Inside and cover art: Ali Howorth
Published by:
Wood Dragon Books
Post Office Box 429
Mossbank, Saskatchewan, Canada S0H3G0
www.wooddragonbooks.com

Available in large print, hardcover, eBook and audiobook

Library and Archives Canada Cataloguing in Publication
Latimer, Deri 1960-
ISBN: 978-1-989078-75-4

Contact the author on email at: deri@derilatimer.com
Or LinkedIn at: https://www.linkedin.com/in/derilatimer/

Contact the artist on Instagram @diamondfishart

Language Warning

There are a number of 'F bombs' in this book.

I decided not to edit out these expletives because it is more authentic to leave them in; they reflect the reality of the voice in my head at the time.

I apologize if you are offended.

I needed to be real.

To Randy, Ali and Max
My heart. My joy. My life.

Contents

HUMAN BLOOMIN'

CHAPTER 1

I'm Human. It was this positive belief about myself that I kept coming back to.

Remembering the thoughts, feelings and behaviors I experienced over the last year is tough. It was real. It was horrendous.

I swore—when I was at my worst—that I would NEVER tell anyone about what I was really thinking, feeling and doing throughout this ordeal.

I changed my mind. And here it is.

NOT CRAZY, *Just Human*

BOO WHO

CHAPTER 2

I grew up in a small mining town in northern Manitoba, the third child (of four) of Helen and Gerry Latimer. If you could beam yourself back to my childhood, you'd see a happy, perky girl who loved to talk and to make people laugh (much to my teachers' chagrin).

I looked up to my older siblings, Dene and Desireé (even though we fought from time to time) and was irritated by my younger sibling, Devin. Pretty normal sibling stuff. By the time we were teenagers, we four had become friends. We liked each other. We hung out together.

In a small town, everyone went to the same parties, many of which were in the bush surrounding our town. (I think that is why I like to camp to this day; and why I crave Baby Duck whenever I am outdoors.) It was not unusual to see the four Latimers all at the same party. I was proud of my siblings and felt privileged to be a part of our family.

I grew up fast. We all did, in the north. By the time I was fourteen, I had already experimented with tobacco, marijuana, had a 'serious' eighteen-year-old boyfriend, and had experienced sex. Yes, you read that right. Not proud of that. When I say I 'experienced sex', it was definitely not all candles and romance. It was my older boyfriend and I with our jeans pulled down, doing the dirty. Pants never came off. You see, we had to be ready to run, in case my mom came around the corner and started chasing us. She spent much of her time stalking and threatening him with bodily injury if he did not stay away from me.

I went away for Grade 12 as my parents really wanted me to have exposure to a larger city and to be challenged in a different school setting. They saw what was happening with the youth in our town (drugs, teen pregnancies, alcohol abuse) and they wanted something different for their children

So, at the age of sixteen, I was driven by my dad to Winnipeg and delivered to the dorm attached to The University of Winnipeg Collegiate. On my first day of class, I walked into Wesley Hall. The castle-like, stately building had me in awe. In the foyer, as we all waited to find out where we were supposed to go, I gasped; I had never seen so many people all in one place in my entire life! In my mind, I stuck out like a sore thumb. Everyone else seemed to be so well dressed, so cool, so citified, and I was wearing my sister's hand-me-downs.

I performed very poorly on the IQ test they gave to us that first day, so poorly that the Dean of the Collegiate asked to see me in his office. I think he wanted to make sure I was going to be able to handle the workload of a shortened school

year at an institution with very high standards. Although I was disappointed at my test score, I was determined that I was not going to quit; I was going to work hard and show my friends in the north that I could succeed. My determination was fueled by a comment from a supposed friend (I'll call her Sara) just before I left the north. She said that I would never make it in the city, and I'd be back just like everyone else. Sara was one of the ones who had tried to leave and quickly came back to the safety of the town she knew. I decided I was going to show her that I would not only make it, I would excel!

Eight months later, I graduated from the Collegiate as a 'Student of Distinction.' I felt vindicated, metaphorically thumbing my nose at Sara. So there, doubter!

I was not sure what I wanted to do with my life. My dad encouraged me to study Business, but that sounded boring to me. I had done well in sciences, so I decided that I would take a lab technology course in Saskatchewan. Why on earth I thought that was a good decision escapes me now. Bodily fluids make me gag.

Two days before I was to leave for college, my dad suffered a massive coronary. It was the day before New Year's Eve in 1978. We were all enjoying the evening at home; Dene and his new wife Debbie (who joined us for dinner before returning to their apartment), Desireé, Devin, myself, Mom, and Dad. Visiting from Lynn Lake were Uncle Ron and Grandma (Dad's brother and mom).

Dad was in a jovial mood. He'd had a few shots of rye (his salve from the stress of his job as Pit Superintendent at the local mine) and there were lots of laughs and lots of food. To prepare to cheer in 1979 the next evening, we all retired early. Desireé, Devin and I slept in the living room on a couple of pull-out couches, and Uncle Ron and Grandma were able to enjoy the privacy of our bedrooms.

In the middle of the night, Mom screamed. "Gerry, wake up! Gerry, WAKE UP!"

I ran down the hallway and I caught a glimpse of my dad. My uncle had my dad sitting up and he was slapping my dad, trying to wake him. Dad was slumped over and not responding at all. After several minutes—maybe even half an hour—Mom asked me to call a neighbor who was a nurse. Betty came over in her pajamas and started to perform CPR on dad. Mom had already called for an ambulance and we were grateful to have Betty there as we awaited its arrival. Mom also asked us to call Dene and he and Debbie rushed over from their apartment.

Dene called the ambulance again. (In Leaf Rapids, the ambulance was run by volunteers. When you called, the connection is transferred directly to the on-call driver's home. At 2:00 a.m., you are likely waking him or her up.) We wanted to make sure that Bob knew this was an emergency situation, and were shocked that he was still at home. "I can't get my car started, can someone there give me a lift to the station?" asked Bob. It had already been 45 minutes since our first call. Dene rushed out to pick up Bob and take him to the fire station, where the ambulance was kept. Another hour passed. Finally, when they arrived, Dene told us that they could not get the ambulance started and Dene had to boost it. It was now two hours past the first sign of distress from my dad. Betty was becoming exhausted. Then Bob informed us that his one and only oxygen tank was empty. Betty moved everyone into action. She knew we had to get Dad to the hospital. She kept doing CPR on him as Dene, Uncle Ron and Bob loaded Dad on the stretcher.

I was both frozen and numb, watching this all unveil. I have a clear image of my dad being wheeled out on the gurney. Mom and Dene went with Betty and Bob to the hospital.

While they were gone, Desireé, Devin and I talked about how we were all going to help out more with shoveling snow, mowing the lawn, and doing repairs around the house. Dad had shoveled our driveway that morning, and we all noticed that he looked exhausted right after he was done. *We will all pitch in and help Dad from now on!*

Three hours later, Mom and Dene returned. "He's gone," Mom said. I remember hearing Devin scream "No!"

The following hours were filled with lots of tears. We couldn't even talk much. We mostly just sobbed. A few years later, Mom told Desireé, Devin and I that Betty was so exhausted in the ambulance on the way to the hospital that she asked Dene to take over giving Dad CPR. Mom said that a gush of blood came out of Dad's mouth when Dene was giving CPR, and that Dene just kept going. I often thought, over the ensuing years, just how difficult that must have been for my brother. He was only 21 years old.

There was a large funeral held in Lynn Lake to honor our dad. We all sat up front and wept. Recently, my brother, Devin, and I talked about how our family never truly talked about Dad's death. No one checked in with Dene to make sure he was okay after what he experienced. Devin was only fourteen and no one reached out to soothe him. We were all broken and struggled with our own grief, privately and individually. Of course, we talked about the funeral and about what we thought Dad's wishes for burial were. Nick, one of my Dad's friends, was the funeral director in town, and he helped Mom tremendously. Although we checked in with each other, it was clear that we were ill-equipped and uncomfortable to have anything other than perfunctory conversation.

Our mom always tried to be so positive and strong. I think she thought it was expected of her; that she had to be strong for us. So, we all 'sucked it up' and moved on with our lives. Only now do I fully appreciate how apt the expression is. We sucked up our emotions and stuffed them deep down inside. We all wanted to be brave for everyone else. Yet the attempt at bravery, the false armor that we wore, actually made us more vulnerable.

I didn't head to college to examine body matter. Instead, I stayed with Mom in Leaf Rapids for the next year so she could get her bearings and not be alone. Dene was married and working in Leaf Rapids and Desireé returned to university in Brandon. Mom thought it would be best to send Devin to live with Desireé in Brandon and attend Grade 10 there. Primarily, Mom was looking out for Devin. If he stayed in Leaf Rapids, he was likely on a path of trouble. Many youth got into drugs and petty crime, and Mom wanted to intercept that path for Devin.

It all happened so fast. I felt bad for Devin. He lost his dad and his mom in one fell swoop.

The next year, I was accepted in the University of Lethbridge's Management Studies Program. I worked hard, barely leaving my dorm room other than to attend classes. It was a day of pride for me when I completed my degree in the four years

required, and achieved Honors status, majoring in Human Resource Management. I also held down two part-time jobs while at university. One in Student Services as a Clerk, and the other with the Student's Union, working at the pub. I definitely spent more time behind the bar serving drinks than I did partaking in all the fun at the pub. It didn't bother me. I was on a mission to make sure I graduated. When I saw my name on the list of Honor Students, I was very proud. The girl from the small northern town had done alright.

During my time at school, Mom moved to Winnipeg and started her first job in over 30 years. The first couple of years after the move were challenging for her. I became her sounding board, her counselor of sorts. We spent hours on the phone. Each school break when I came home to visit, we went for long walks and talked and talked. Although she loved all her children and each was special to her in their own way, I knew I was important to Mom not only as a daughter, but as her trusted friend. I was glad to be that support for her and we became very close, a bond that lasted for the rest of her life.

When I graduated in April of 1984, I got a sweet job at a new startup company where I staffed the company from three to over 200. It was very exciting. One day after work, my friend and roommate, Karen, and I went out to a club. Within the first hour of arriving, I saw a most delicious man sitting at the next table and we locked eyes. Eventually, he made his way over to our table, and Kelly and I spent the rest of the night together, talking and laughing.

The next day, I travelled to Winnipeg for Christmas. I told my family all about this cute guy I met at a bar. We exchanged phone numbers that night in the bar, and I just hoped that he would call me when I returned in the new year. He did. And we spent every day together after that.

We married a year after we met and moved to Calgary. Kelly registered for a course to become a Sound Technician and I was able to get a great job with the Energy Resources Conservation Board as an Employee Relations Specialist. When Kelly graduated, he soon discovered that finding a job in that field was very challenging, and the promise made by the organization through which he took the course to help him find work did not come to fruition. After months of looking for work, he decided to go back to school and upgrade his skills (he had to complete his GED first since he was missing one credit from high school) so he could follow in his mom's footsteps by becoming an X-ray Technologist.

It was hard on him. Academia was not his forte.

With his studies and my work, sometimes we were like ships passing in the night. We started writing notes to each other, as a way to connect and to share information where we needed to do so. It was always so fun to come home and find a new note waiting on the kitchen table. Most of the time they were really funny (and a tad erotic).

Eight months into our marriage, I arrived at our apartment after a day at work, and saw a note on the table. I smiled, thinking it was one of his cute or sexy messages. But it wasn't.

It read:

Der,

I can't control my life anymore
I'm a drug addict
I wish you never met me
please forgive me

Love, kel

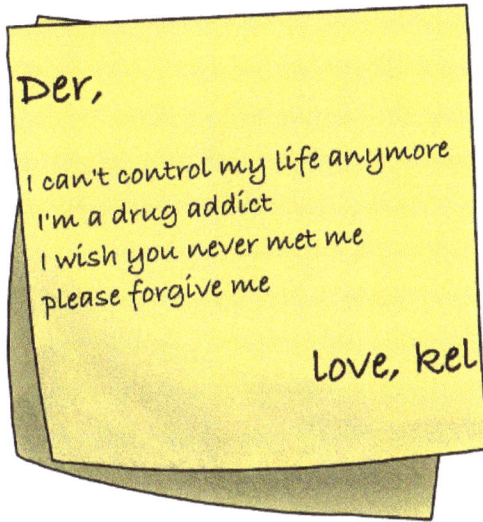

I stared at it, half expecting him to come around the corner and tell me it was all a joke.

I ran through the apartment looking for him. I looked out of our 10th story window and noticed that his car was gone. I read and re-read the note. Then, the panic set in. Oh my god, what is happening? *Kelly, what is happening?*

I called my mom and then my sister. I was hysterical. Desireé just said, "I am on my way." She and her then boyfriend, Carlos, jumped in her car and drove from Winnipeg to Calgary.

I called Kelly's brother, Gary, who lived in Calgary. Their father, Walter, was in Calgary visiting from Pincher Creek and decided to stay in the city upon hearing this news about Kelly.

Gary was understandably concerned. He asked me a ton of questions like, "Was something going on between the two of you?" and "'Did you notice anything strange about him in the last few days?"

I answered, "No" to them all. I knew nothing. To me, everything had been normal.

Yes, I told Gary, Kelly was finding his courses challenging. But he seemed to be doing just fine and was working really hard to complete his studies.

As I waited for Desireé to arrive, I called a Suicide Hot Line. I was desperate for help. I felt so confused and alone. They asked me questions too, and they were glad that my sister was on the way to be with me.

I called my boss and told her the situation. She said to take as much time as I needed.

When Desireé arrived, she went into detective mode. She tore through all of Kelly's things, looking for anything she could find that might help us understand what secrets he might have been hiding and where he might be.

After an hour, she emerged with a notebook that was among his school books. Near the back of the notebook there was a list that read: Flight, hotel, booze, go out with a bang. I was stunned. And even more frightened. It was now clear that he had planned this.

I could not sleep, so finally at 3:00 in the morning, Desireé took me to the emergency department at Calgary Foothills Hospital. The doctor prescribed sleeping pills. When we arrived back at the apartment, I took a pill and washed it down with vodka. I had no appetite. I had no strength.

My brother Dene arrived the next day. I remember him embracing me as I sobbed and sobbed. He lay down with me after I took my sleeping pill and hugged me until it kicked in. I kept asking him what I had done to make Kelly do this. My

beautiful brother just held me and comforted me and assured me that I had done nothing to make this happen.

Devin was travelling through Europe at the time and, in those days before cell phones, we had no immediate way to reach him. We had to wait until the next time he called home.

We called the Calgary police and reported Kelly missing. The sergeant who took the report informed us that, because Kelly was an adult, he had a right to disappear, and that if they found him, they could only tell him that we were concerned for him, they could not make him come home.

The next day, Officer James came to the apartment to meet with me. He noticed the sleeping pills on the counter. He picked them up and asked me to follow him to the bathroom. "Dump them in, Deri," he said. "You do not want to get addicted to those. I have seen it happen too many times. This is a very difficult situation for you, I know, but this is not a solution." (I still, thirty-three years later, thank Officer James for telling me to dump those pills.)

My boss, Diane, came over on night two and took me out to drive around the downtown of Calgary, hoping to get a glimpse of Kelly's car. Desireé and I drove around the airport parking lot, thinking Kelly's car might be there.

Desireé soon became the main communicator with our family and with Kelly's family. I was a zombie. I refused to leave our apartment because I wanted to be there when Kelly came back, or in case he called. I sat on the couch beside the phone and waited.

Finally, on day seven, Desireé convinced me to leave the apartment to go out for coffee. I agreed only because she bought me an answering machine. Just in case Kelly called.

When we arrived back at the apartment, the light was flashing. There was a message!

"Desireé. It's Lorna. Call me," was the message. Lorna was Gary's wife.

Desireé called. She listened. Our eyes met, and I knew.

All this while, no one thought to look at Kelly's father's trailer in Pincher Creek. Gary asked one of Kelly's friends to break in, and he found Kelly in his father's bedroom. There was another note there, one expressing his love for us all.

Kelly shot himself using his father's gun. We later were informed by the coroner that Kelly died that first day.

Devin got to Calgary just after the funeral. I was so happy to see him, and also so sad that he had to come home to such awful news.

Devin drove Mom and I to Winnipeg the day after the funeral. I lay in the back seat for almost the entire 12 hours. During our stops, I had difficulty eating.

Devin was my constant companion. We stayed up late at night in Mom's apartment, and talked about Kelly and about how this could have happened. While we found no evidence of Kelly being a drug addict, that is what he wrote in his note so we thought we had to believe it. Devin and I decided that maybe, just maybe, Kelly did not kill himself. Maybe someone else did it. Maybe he owed someone drug money and that was why they killed him.

Within a few weeks of being in Winnipeg, I knew I had to quit my job and move to be closer to my family. Devin and I drove back to Calgary. We donated all of Kelly's clothes, and we sent

everything from the apartment to an auction house to be sold. On our drive back to Winnipeg, we decided to stop into the police department in Pincher Creek. We met with a detective and told him our theory about Kelly's death being a murder rather than a suicide.

He just stared at us. Then he said, "It was a suicide. If you want proof, I can show you the pictures."

"No thank you," we said, and we went on our way. That pretty well took care of our murder theories for good.

Thankfully, I got a job rather shortly after I started looking. That phone call from Doraine Empson offering me a position with Northern Telecom Canada gave me the first sign of hope that I was going to be okay and to recover from losing Kelly.

On my third day of employment with Northern Telecom, I set off to meet the Production Managers on the plant floor. One of my first assignments was to staff 50 entry level and technical positions, and I wanted to meet with each Production Manager to get an understanding of their requirements.

My third meeting was with Randy Howorth. I approached his office and knocked. He turned to greet me with the best smile I'd seen in a long time. "Hi Deri! Nice to meet you! Have a seat." My meetings with the other managers were pretty brief and business-focused. My meeting with Randy was different. He asked me all about my background, and about what brought me to Winnipeg. I told Randy, as I did others who asked, that I was recently widowed and decided to move to Winnipeg to be close to my family. (No one asked how my husband died; I would have lied at that time as I still had not come to terms with the fact that it was a suicide. I could not even say the word.) Randy expressed sincere condolences and then continued to ask about my family. He was interested in me, and it felt good.

I found myself thinking about Randy a lot. I really liked him. A lot. At the same time, I felt like I was cheating on Kelly, being interested in another man. And I knew that my heart was still quite injured. I knew I needed to do some work before I could contemplate any sort of relationship with Randy.

Thankfully, Northern Telecom offered an Employee Assistance Program for all staff. Within the first month of my employment, I booked an appointment to see Dr. Maurice, a psychologist. I was glad that the service was confidential, and that Dr. Maurice's office was structured such that privacy was assured. I was ashamed. Ashamed that my husband died by suicide. Ashamed for being ashamed that my husband died by suicide. Ashamed that I needed help to deal with it. Ashamed that I wanted to be able to move on with my life.

It was tough to make that first call. I have to admit that I was apprehensive to ask for help. As I have shared with you, our family was a 'pick yourself up and dust yourself off' kind of family. Asking for help just didn't happen.

I only saw Dr. Maurice for three appointments. He helped me to reframe my shame, and to understand a little about where the shame came from. As he was getting to know me, I shared about my background growing up in a small, isolated northern community. My father was a rather prominent figure in the community, being one of the highest-ranked leaders at

Sherritt Gordon Mines, the main employer in our community. My mother, a beautiful and graceful woman, was also a notable community member. She single-handedly brought television to the north. In those days, it took diligence and determination. Mom had to write letters to CBC (Canadian Broadcasting Corporation) and to politicians, making a case for why we deserved access to this new medium. Mom also taught dance classes in our basement. She was not a professional dancer, and in fact, had never had a lesson herself. She learned how to do the Highland Fling and Ukrainian Dance (remember, there was no internet, no YouTube, in those days) and offered free lessons to any child who was interested. Of course, the four of us (Dene, Desireé, Devin and myself) were students! Mom engaged with other mothers to offer their talents making costumes for us. When I think back to it now, I am completely amazed at her creativity and energy.

Because our parents were known and respected in the community, Mom had zero tolerance for any behavior on our part that caused her embarrassment. I certainly get it. Small towns can be vicious. Gossip, rampant.

So, when Dr. Maurice connected those dots for me, I could see why I experienced so much shame when Kelly died. I believed I would be judged by others because my husband chose death over life with me. I didn't realize until much later that I was also judging myself.

On our second date, I told Randy the truth about Kelly's death. He was so amazing, so compassionate, so caring. I remember one moment that evening when I looked into his eyes and I knew that I would be with him for the rest of my life.

Randy and I dated, and through him, I met a large group of wonderful friends. We had so much fun meeting for dinner after work, and getting together with friends on the weekends. Life was great and I was truly in love. This love was much deeper and much more authentic than any I had ever experienced.

Two years later, Randy applied for and won a role in the Human Resources Department, the department in which I worked! It was not long before we knew that one of us was going to have to leave; working together and dating was not workable in the long term.

I was happy to leave. Randy already had over ten years of service with Northern Telecom, and I had my sights set on self-employment. I met two consultants, Steve Davis and Gordon Dale, who we had hired on a few occasions to work with our leaders, and I knew that I wanted to do what they were doing. One evening, I took them out for dinner, and asked if I might be able to work with them in their business. They said, "Yes!" with the caveat that they couldn't pay me. I would only be paid for any work that I got on my own.

Luckily, within a week of my leaving Northern Telecom and joining Davis, Dale and Associates, I landed a contract with CN Rail to join a team of trainers rolling out a leadership program across the country. It was amazing! Ten of us gathered in Whistler, BC, to learn the program and practice delivering it. We were paired up with a senior leader at CN, one who we would work with for the next two years delivering this program. I was paired with Rob Weir, and to this day, I have fond memories of our spirited conversations! I had the university education and Rob had the real-world leadership experience. Together, we were a great team!

Shortly after I started my self-employment, Randy and I moved in together. A year and a half later, on my birthday in December of 1992, Randy proposed, and we began planning our wedding for September 4, 1993.

I had changed my name when I married Kelly, and still had Karp as my surname. Randy and I discussed that I would change my name when we got married, and that I would go back to my birth name, Latimer.

Our wedding day was so much fun! We decided to forgo many of the usual trappings, such as cake and flowers. We kept it simple. I had my dress made by a local designer, a simple and funky number, paired with gold shoes (white ones that I painted!), huge gold hoop earrings, and my mom's gold handbag. Randy donned a stunning tuxedo. We were joined at the alter by family and friends. On my side were my sister, Desireé, sister-in-law, Debbie, soon-to-be-sister-in-law, Cindy, and friend, Sheila. On Randy's side were his brothers, Herb and Gord, and his childhood friends, Paul and Rob. The wedding guests were, likewise, family and friends and we danced and laughed all night. It was glorious!

We left the day after the wedding for a three-week honeymoon in Greece. We came back with an extra package; I was expecting our first child.

Ali Latimer Howorth was born on June 3, 1994 (exactly nine months after our wedding). I was 33 and Randy was 35. We were so ready to be parents!

I knew I wanted to be at home with Ali, so although I stayed connected to Steve and Gord, we did no further work together. I did take on some work that I could do from home, helping friends with their resumes, typing up documents for my friend in real estate, odds and ends that I could do when Ali was napping. I loved (and still love) being a mom.

When Ali was a year old, I applied to teach in the Management Studies Program at The University of Winnipeg's Professional and Continuing Education Division. I knew I had something to offer, and I felt a true calling to teach. I also knew that this was work that I could do in the evenings. So, for a couple of years, I was able to teach a class here and there, while Randy was at home with Ali. During that time, I was offered an opportunity to do some training with the Government of Manitoba and with the Worker's Compensation Board of Manitoba.

Through a friend, I met Cathy Creran, who was available to care for Ali on an occasional basis, so that I could do some contract training. I loved the idea of Ali being in the care of a warm, loving woman who had only one other child in her care, my friend's son, Joshua. It allowed Ali some play time and it allowed me a chance to develop my business as a speaker, trainer and consultant.

When Ali was 2 ½, the three of us travelled to the north. There was a reunion in Leaf Rapids that I wanted to attend, and then we travelled to Lynn Lake to visit my grandma and uncle. One day, I felt nauseas and tired. I thought it was due to the heat, it was unseasonably warm that summer. When we got back to Winnipeg, I found the source. I was pregnant with our second child.

Max Randolph Howorth was born on March 28, 1997. A strapping boy at 9 lbs. 11 oz., he seemed to do nothing but sleep for the first two months of his life. Ali was my little helper and they were the cutest pair as they grew up together. I loved, loved, loved motherhood. At the same time, I continued to develop my speaking business, and I learned that having meaningful work truly added to my mothering. Everything I learned about human communication, wellness, resilience, happiness, I wanted to be able to share with Ali and Max. Every keynote I created, I created for them. They weren't in the

audience, of course, but I wanted to contribute meaningfully and positively to a world that was filled with resilient and well humans. For them.

In 2012, a colleague (and now dear friend, Jennifer, who you will hear more about later) nominated me to deliver a TEDx talk. "You have to tell your story, Deri. People need to hear it." I had never publicly talked about Kelly's suicide. My friends and family knew, some clients knew, but I did not make it central to the messages I delivered on resilience and wellbeing. I knew it was time to 'come out'! It was time for many reasons. Mental health was becoming a mainstream topic. And, I was very concerned about my older brother, Dene.

I had always had a special relationship with Dene. I was close to him and his wife, Debbie, and I saw them often, even though they lived in Ontario. On my 40th birthday, in 2000, Debbie called me and said that Dene was not doing well. He had an argument with his manager, and had been demoted from his supervisory role, back to the role of electrician. He had been laying on the couch, facing the back, for three days. Debbie wanted me to talk to Dene. She knew I read a lot and spoke on topics related to positive mental health.

When Dene got on the phone, I could tell that he was very sad. "I messed up. There is nothing I can do. It's over. I messed up." I tried to reassure him, I encouraged him to reach out to his manager, maybe there was something that could be done to rectify the situation. "It's over, Deri. I messed up and that is that."

Over the next 13 years, Dene was up and down. He worked

really hard to feel better, and did what his doctors suggested. Sometimes, he was incapable of working. Other times, he excelled, and even travelled to exotic locations, like Thailand and Indonesia, leading electrical projects for mining contractors. He was always so proud of his sons, Michael and Jeffrey, and when he felt good, he made sure to spend tons of time with them.

In 2013, I prepared for what would become the most important talk of my life. Dene was not well. I was worried about his wellbeing, and about what might happen to him. His marriage was all but over, and he was often tough to reach by telephone. He had just left a rehabilitation facility earlier than suggested and I truly feared we might lose him.

My TEDx talk is called 'Choose Life'. In 14:38 (64 seconds under the maximum 15 minutes), I told the story of Kelly's suicide for the first time in public, and I told it through the lens of the night I told Ali and Max (who were just 8 and 11 at the time I told them). From the second I held Ali and Max in my arms, I knew I would one day have to tell them about this dark part of my life. I finally did it the night before I was about to be interviewed on a radio program. I thought this might come out in the interview, and I wanted Ali and Max to hear it from me directly. I also shared in the TEDx talk, without naming him because I did not have his permission, a bit about Dene and my interpretation of what I thought was going on for him.

I practiced for hours. During each practice, 50-60 of them, I choked up, especially remembering the night I told Ali and Max about Kelly. I did not want to choke up on stage, fearing it might kill the whole talk. I still have a record of the multiple

versions of the talk that I prepared and practiced and the 24 recorded versions on my laptop. I was never so ready to deliver a talk, and I was also never so nervous. I wasn't sure I could get through it.

I did choke, but only at the very end of the talk. Only in the last sentence I delivered. I invited the audience to stay curious, caring and connected with others. To take a moment in their busy lives to really see people around them, because that other person might be suffering and in need of help. When I said, "It might just save a life, maybe even your own," I was thinking about Dene.

Walking out into the reception area after the talk, I was swarmed by people from the audience. Many were crying and thanking me for sharing my message. It astounded me how many people had experienced either a suicide or a family member who was struggling in some way; with addiction, eating disorders, anxiety, or depression. I was so happy in that moment, and so grateful to have had the opportunity to tell some of my story, with the hope of helping others. *Okay, I've got this! I've shared the biggest 'secret' I have and I feel great for having done it.* I was determined to show that personal traumas, struggles, could turn into opportunities for growth. I knew this would be a pivotal moment in my life, and in my professional speaking career.

Later that summer, Dene moved to Winnipeg from Collingwood, Ontario. He got a bachelor's apartment in the same building in which my mother had lived, and he began his life here. Shortly after arriving, he secured contracted employment with various mining contractors within Manitoba.

Desireé, Devin and I were thrilled to have our big brother so close to us. Dene was well and happy!! He was very close with both of his sons, and communicated with them often. Michael lived in Collingwood with his wife, Krystal, and three children, Hudson, Landon and Charlee. Jeffrey and his girlfriend Natalie lived in Winnipeg.

In 2017, we hosted a Latimer family reunion at our cottage, just after Jeffrey and Natalie's wedding. There were 30 of us all together, and we spent the weekend boating, tubing, water-skiing, swimming, eating, and laughing. Dene was so happy! Each morning he was in charge of getting coffee going, and each morning I was one of the first to join him. Those early morning coffee chats were some of the highlights of that weekend for me.

On October 7, 2018, we were told that our beautiful mom, who had been living with dementia for over 10 years, was entering the last few days of her life. Mom had developed an infection, and without hospitalization, she would die. Mom's health care directive was for comfort care only. We did not want Mom to suffer, and we also knew Mom would not want to keep living the way she had been; trapped in a mind and body that no longer worked. We all had been able to visit her regularly. In fact, we looked forward to each visit. Even though Mom really could not communicate with us for most of those 10 years, we loved to get together and visit there, and we believed Mom could hear us. Although she did not know, she actually brought us closer together through those visits.

On October 11, 2018, I visited Mom alone. It was 5:00 a.m. and Unit C, where Mom lived, was dark and quiet. I slipped into her room and took her hand, as I had so many times before. I was leaving at 8:00 a.m. for a five-day business trip, and I was pretty sure this was the last time I would see, and touch, my mom. I told her I loved her and that I was so grateful that

she was my mom. I kissed her and hugged her on my way out, imprinting the feel of her soft, warm skin in my memory.

Dene called me late that evening. "She's gone," he said. I sat on the edge of the bed in my hotel room and thought about those words ... *She's gone*. I did not cry. I was not really sure what I felt. Part of what I felt was a sense of peace, happy that my mom was finally free.

I had an early keynote presentation the next morning, and I knew it was 'game on'; I had to set aside the fact that my mom just died, and 'get on with the show'.

By the time I got back to Winnipeg after that trip, Mom had already been cremated, and much of what needed to be done to settle her estate was in process. We celebrated Mom's life with a small family gathering, and watched old home movies from our lives growing up.

There was Mom, always the picture of beauty and grace. Always smiling. I remember watching one video from a family trip to visit Dad's relatives in Saskatchewan in 1966. There were Desireé and I, decked out in matching bathing suits and cute summer hats. Dene frolicked with our cousins who were close in age to him, and Devin ran in and out of the water, splashing himself. And there was Mom, looking like a movie star. I can only imagine the reality of that moment. It would have been so stressful for my mom. She was not a swimmer and did not like water. There was chaos all around, kids running around, adults standing around chatting. I am sure if I could have peeked into Mom's mind, she would have been wishing it was all over because she'd be so worried about one of us drowning. But there was Mom getting 'on with the show'.

On March 19, 2019, I texted Dene to meet for coffee the next day. No response. I waited a few hours and texted again. Still nothing. I tried one more time: *Hey, bro, where are you? Should I send out the posse?* When I didn't hear back, I got really worried.

I texted my sister and Dene's son, Jeffrey: *Have you heard from Dene?*

No, they both texted back.

We all rushed over to Dene's apartment building. We told the apartment manager that we were worried about Dene. We knocked on his door and it was quiet inside. The apartment manager tried to use her master key, but the chain lock was engaged. That meant that Dene was inside.

We called the police, who arrived within minutes of the call. They asked us to wait outside of the apartment while they kicked the door in and entered the suite. We (Desireé, Jeffrey, Natalie and I) stood frozen in the hallway for the longest five minutes of our lives.

"It looks like he went in his sleep," the officer said. I do not remember much about that moment, except that I saw Jeffrey fall forward and I fell right into him. We were all sobbing. We entered the apartment and there was Dene, curled up in bed and looking like he was sleeping.

"Oh, Dene, oh, Dene, oh, Dene," was all I could say. I kissed him and he was very cold.

DERI LATIMER

The officers told us to go out for coffee for a couple of hours so the coroner could do what he needed to do.

I called Randy and he called Ali and Max. Desireé called Keri, Devin's wife, and she called Devin, who was on a father/daughter trip with Hazel at the time.

I sat in the restaurant, but could not talk, drink coffee, or even see very clearly. Suddenly, I said, "I think I will go home. I'm not going to be much help to any of you right now. I'll see you tomorrow."

I got lost walking to my car. I was disoriented and couldn't see because I was sobbing. In hindsight, I shouldn't have driven home.

I arrived and fell into Randy's arms. We all (Randy, Ali, Max and I) sat around our kitchen table and I told them what happened. As they had responded when I told Ali and Max about Kelly 14 years earlier, they showed their love and compassion toward me through their eyes and their soothing voices. Ali put her hand on mine.

Randy and Max had a trip to Vegas planned, and they were to leave the next morning. Ali was also going to be out of town. "We will cancel our trip," Randy said.

"No," I said. "Please go, I will be alright." And, I knew I would be. After all, I'd been through some bad stuff before. I can do this. I also knew that I would want to be near Jeffrey, who just lost his father. I wanted to be there as a support for him and to help in any way I could.

We celebrated Dene's life a few weeks later, when Michael was able to make it into town. We held it at the Thistle Curling Club, where Dene spent many hours curling with Devin,

Jeffrey, Keri and Ryan (Desireé's son-in-law). He loved it there!

Jeffrey asked me to say a few words at the celebration. I prepared a short speech, knowing I could never say all that I wanted to say about my wonderful brother. Michael and Jeffrey opened by sharing some of Dene's memorable sayings (like 'tighter than a bull's arse at fly time' to describe anything that was, well, tight!), causing everyone to laugh through our tears. I made it through my speech with a few tears in tow, and I kept it light and funny, since that is exactly the kind of human our brother was. Pure Joy.

Losing Dene so close to losing Mom was overwhelming. And yet, in true Latimer fashion, we got up and dusted ourselves off and carried on with our lives. We had to move on. Of course, we talk about Dene, Mom and Dad all the time, mostly sharing the funny memories we have of them. When Devin and I talk about Dene, we inevitably get choked up. Just gracing the edge of our grief is too distressing to stay there for too long. So, we move through the moment quickly, and then change the subject. On with the show.

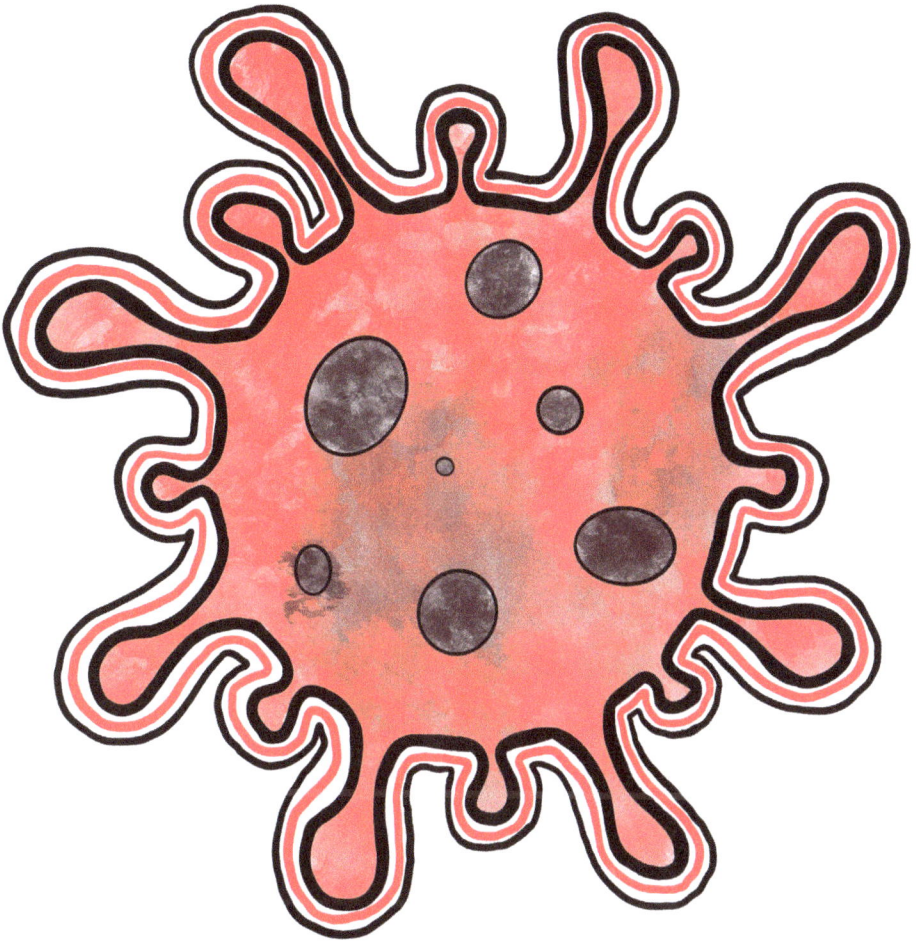

PANDEMIC PANIC

CHAPTER 3

As we lay on the beach in Huatulco, Mexico, on the second day of our one-week vacation in March of 2020, Randy's phone started blowing up with voice mail messages from his panicked HR Director in Chicago. "I don't know what to do. A pandemic has been declared and people are asking all sorts of questions. Do we send them home? Do we stop travel completely? For those who need to go into hospitals to maintain our equipment, will be provide danger pay? How about PPE? Do we allow visitors into the office?" The HR Director in Winnipeg was not at all panicked, and had, actually, barely heard about the pandemic. Randy wasn't sure what to believe. I know him to be a very logical, thoughtful person. He can handle pressure very well, and maintain his composure. I could see that this situation was causing him great concern. And, it certainly concerned me.

The panicked calls continued for the next few days. I found myself heading to the gym or the beach by myself as Randy managed the situation from afar—with very little information and, of course, no prior experience of leading an organization's people and culture through a global pandemic.

By the end of day five, I just wanted to get on a plane and go home. The pandemic was just about all anyone could talk about at the resort. Ali and Max called, saying they were told to stay home and that they would be completing their post-secondary studies remotely.

We tried to get a flight out early, but Huatulco had only one flight per week to Winnipeg, so we had to wait for our originally scheduled return flight. Each time I heard a guest talking to hotel staff about trying to arrange for an early check out, I wanted to just get going. The morning of our departure, I was ready super-early with packed suitcases at the door, before Randy even woke for the day. Thank goodness Randy is patient. I wanted to get to the lobby early, check out early, get on the bus early—I just wanted to be gone.

That day was the first day I saw people wearing masks. Many of the hotel staff were masked, and all airport personnel were masked. It was so strange. I didn't realize at the time—I did not name it—but I was experiencing fear, which I pushed away because acknowledging the fear was too frightening.

Once at the airport, I was relieved and excited to be that much closer to getting home. I noticed a good-looking couple at the airport. We were behind them in line going through security. They both were wearing funky clothes and had great shoes, casual and expensive-looking at the same time! I remember admiring the couple and wondering what their life was like, what kind of house they lived in, who their friends were. This game is one that I have played since childhood, a part

of my 'tendency to daydream' that teachers always noted in my report cards. I wonder about people, sometimes I even make up stories about them. I noticed then that his suitcase said "Willard Reaves", which did not mean anything to me. I whispered to Randy and asked if he knew anyone by that name, being we were all headed to Winnipeg. Randy told me that Reaves was a former Running Back for the Winnipeg Blue Bombers.

As we sat waiting for our flight to be called, a woman approached me. "Deri?" she asked.

I looked at her and knew that I knew her, but could not remember from where or what her name was. I said, "Yes, hi!" giving her a little hug and pretending I knew her name and hoping that I'd figure it out after a few seconds of chatting.

"Oh, I guess we aren't supposed to do that!" she said after our hello-hug.

"Yes, I guess so," I responded. The 'wash your hands, don't touch your face, social distance' warnings were all over the media at that point in time.

Finally, our flight was boarding. I noticed that Brenda and Willard Reaves were just ahead of me in line. Then, low and behold, they were seated beside me—he at the window, she in the middle seat and me on the aisle. I noticed Brenda wiping down her table and armrests, and she kindly offered me one of her Lysol wipes.

I took it and thanked her. "You must be the only one with wipes on this plane." I said. "Yes, I think you are right", Brenda replied.

We'd already started hearing about shortages of wipes, sanitizer, and toilet paper. On the plane, I prepared a shopping list for Ali and Max. Our plan was to send them to Costco once we got home. Loaded with those supplies, we would trade in our beachwear clothing for winter wear and head to our cottage for our two-week mandatory isolation.

ISOLATION SITUATION

CHAPTER 4

My habit, 5-6 times a week (unless I was travelling for work), was to arise at 4:45 a.m. and head to the gym. There was a regular group of 6 a.m.'ers who did the same, and we formed a little community that I value highly. Nine years ago, I started going in to the gym ahead of the class, so that I could get a little extra work-out in. On days when the class was a weight class, I would do cardio on the treadmill or elliptical. On days when the class was cardio, I would do some muscle work before the class. I felt strong and fit, and I loved how I felt each morning as I left the gym at 7 a.m. I was energized and ready for the day!

At the cottage, for the first few days of self-isolation, I was glued to my computer. Randy was working long hours and I was trying to keep up with the news and returning emails.

One by one, my speaking engagements were cancelled, rescheduled or postponed until further notice.

I noticed that my energy was low, and I was simultaneously feeling agitated. I thought I would start getting back into my habit of an early morning workout. I asked Randy to see what he had in the garage that I could use for weights. He found a couple of axe heads and duct-taped some metal pieces to them. Voila! I had weights.

Each morning I got up and headed downstairs to work out. YouTube was my friend, and I quickly found a few instructors that I liked. The 6 a.m.'ers formed an email chain and started sharing stories of what workouts they were doing. One of our main instructors at the gym is Roxy. She is young, energetic, beautiful, and a work-out beast! When I got to the gym, generally at 5:15 a.m., she was already running on the treadmill and covered in sweat. Roxy mentioned to our group that Mossa Fitness was offering free online workouts. I tried them and really enjoyed them. I got a good sweat on and the workouts were a perfect length at 30 minutes. I did those workouts twice a day, every day while we were isolating, and even now, 14 months later, I can hear the music and recite the instructions verbatim.

I felt good immediately after the workout, but the feeling did not last. Throughout the day, I felt worse and worse.

I must need more social interaction, I thought. Randy was consumed with work and by the time his work day was done, he was pretty well exhausted. I set up a zoom chat with 'the girls', a group of eight women who have been friends for over twenty years. Shortly after I moved to Winnipeg in 1988, I met Randy's sister, Cindy. Through Cindy, I met Cathy, Joanne, Cindy V, Wendy, Marcy, Cheri and Sharon. We had a regular ritual of getting together to drink wine, eat appetizers and open

birthday presents as we rotated turns. I really missed the girls.

Our zoom chat was great. It was so good to hear about how everyone was doing and how they were filling their time as most of us were either isolating or working remotely. Sharon was the only one working full time as a Nurse in Leduc, Alberta. Thankfully, her hospital had no COVID cases through the whole pandemic. She did, however, share her concerns about the increase in people experiencing mental health challenges.

I also set up regular zooms with my very good friends through CAPS (Canadian Association of Professional Speakers). Suzanne and Jennifer were, like me, wondering how to 'pivot' to the new reality of virtual speaking. They were actually more than wondering, they were doing it! I loved hearing about all of the equipment they were acquiring and the studios they were building in their homes. Even though I loved to hear what they were doing, I had no motivation to do it myself. *I am sure this will pass and we'll get back to normal* was my quiet mantra to myself.

During our isolation, we drove from the Cottage to our home in Winnipeg to celebrate our son Max's 23rd birthday on March 28th. We stayed apart and did not hug or touch each other in any way. It was so weird, but we wanted to be safe. Both Ali and Max were working in front-line jobs, and although Randy and I had not seen another human for 11 days, Ali and Max were regularly working with the public. Although it was strange celebrating under these COVID restrictions, I have fond memories of that day. One when my brother, Devin, and his family, Keri, Hazel and Oscar surprised Max by coming over and singing Happy Birthday to him from our driveway. Little did we know at the time that the 'driveway visit' would become part of our new normal.

I slowly realized that if I was going to keep out of an agitated state, it would take more than one socially-distanced visit with my children and a handful of Zoom calls. I needed a system, a routine. I decided to create a checklist.

To do
Work out ✓
Peruse the newspaper ✓
meditate ✓
Do yoga ✓
Solve a sudoku ✓
Work on a puzzle ✓
Take a walk ✓
Connect with a friend ✓
Write in journal ✓

Still, I continued to feel 'off'. I forced myself through my morning workout, while my legs and arms started to feel like they weighed 100 lbs. each. It was a chore. I thought maybe switching up the workout or trying new instructors might help.

It didn't.

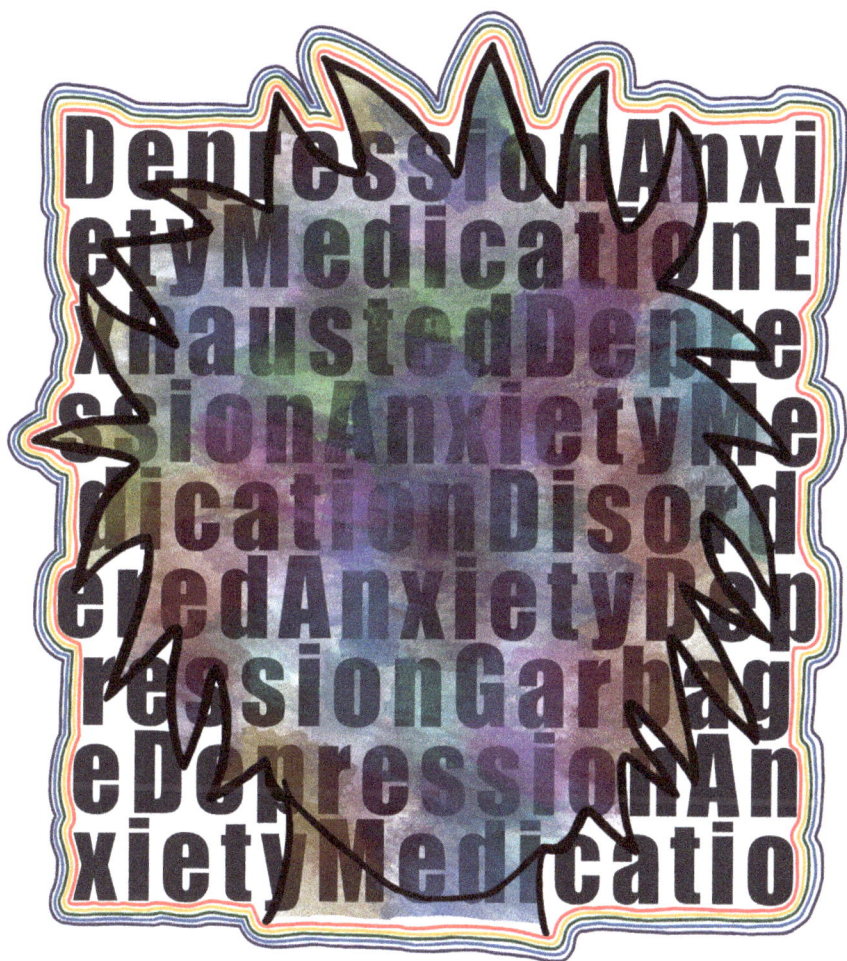

SLEEP CREEP

CHAPTER 5

I was having restless sleeps. *That must be why I feel so bad*, I thought. I had some Zopiclone tablets, which my doctor had prescribed years ago to take every now and then when I found the effects of peri-menopause had impacted my sleep. That little blue pill always did the trick, and I never felt drowsy.

I started taking the half tablet of Zopiclone at bedtime because I was really feeling exhausted. Then, I increased to a full tablet, then one and a half, then two. I started to run short on tablets and was also concerned about how much I could safely take.

I called my family physician, Dr. Suffia Ahmad. In those early pandemic days, it was a chore to try to get an appointment. Finally, it was set for six days later and it was to be a phone call. Those were a long six days. I told Dr. Ahmad that I wasn't sleeping and that I felt terrible. I asked if she could prescribe me more Zopiclone and she confirmed that I could take up to three pills, if necessary.

The new prescription did not help. Not only was I still not sleeping, but I was feeling like complete garbage. The days were very long. I stopped drinking coffee and all alcohol intake. I made myself work out and go for walks. Nothing seemed to help. I also could not focus on anything. I could not read, work on a puzzle, or watch a movie. I lost interest in connecting with people, but forced myself to interact, none-the-less.

I called Dr. Ahmad's office again, and again waited several days to set up another phone call. It went like this:

Me: The Zopiclone is not working and I feel really bad.

Dr. A: Bad in what way, what are you noticing?

Me: It is hard to describe but I have no energy and I can't focus.

Dr. A: Let's get some bloodwork done, to see what might be going on.

I had researched my symptoms and convinced myself that the problem was my thyroid. *Great, maybe she can just give me a pill to fix it and I can get back to normal,* I thought.

Again, I waited. Five days later, I called Dr. Ahmad's office to get the results. "Your bloodwork was normal, nothing is showing up as a concern," she said.

I swore under my breath. I was hoping I could just take a pill and be better.

"I need to see you in person," she continued.

I called the office and set up an appointment. It was for two weeks later. A. Very. Long. Two. Weeks.

By the time my appointment arrived, I was a mess. We were back at home in Winnipeg; Randy was working at our kitchen table, Ali was studying downstairs, and Max was studying upstairs. And I was barely existing. I tried to act 'normal', especially around the kids. I did not want to worry them or to distract them from their studies. But Randy knew I was not good. (Of course, in hindsight, I also know that Ali and Max knew there was something up with Mom.)

By the time I saw Dr. Ahmad in person, I was very thin and my clothing hung loosely. I was not working out regularly, and my muscle mass was quickly disappearing. When I looked at myself in the mirror as I was getting into the shower, I was horrified. I looked like a skeleton. A really old, frightened skeleton.

I asked Randy to come with me to my doctor's appointment. I was not sure that I could drive, and I also was not sure I could communicate properly once there. Luckily, the receptionist let Randy come in with me; even though the protocol was to attend appointments alone. I asked for an exception, and she granted it. I think she could see the desperation in my eyes.

Dr. Ahmad asked a bunch of questions. I told her that I was experiencing an increased heart rate on a regular basis. I found wearing a mask made it hard to breathe, and that elevated my panicky/antsy feeling. She ordered more bloodwork and an EKG. Having lost both my father and my brother to heart attacks, I thought that seemed like a good idea.

All tests came back normal.

Dr. Ahmad asked Randy a number of questions. She needed to

understand what was 'normal' for me, since I was a relatively new client of hers. He confirmed that I was definitely not myself.

"Deri, we have thoroughly checked you out from a physical standpoint, and there is nothing showing up. I don't have one of these," she said, pointing to the blood pressure indicator beside her desk, "that I can use to check you out mentally. All I can do is guess, and my guess is that you are experiencing symptoms of anxiety and you require medication."

I just stared at her. *Really?* I thought. *Can I really feel this shitty from anxiety? What do I have to be anxious about anyway? I have a great life, a great family, lots of friends. WTF?!*

"I am going to prescribe a different sleeping aid, called Trazodone. We have to get you sleeping. We will start at a half tablet for five days, then increase to one tablet. I want to see you in two weeks."

Even though when I thought it was my thyroid, I was hoping I could just get a pill and feel better, somehow the thought of taking a pill for anxiety repelled me. Needing help for a mental concern seemed like a sign of weakness. I was surprised by this realization, that somewhere deep down I had some judgement about needing help and not just being able to 'get over it'.

Reading the drug information sheet on Trazodone freaked me out! I had to read and re-read it thanks to my lack of lack of focus.

> **Your mental health may change in unexpected ways when you take trazodone or other antidepressants.** *(What? I am not depressed! I cannot be depressed!)*

You may become suicidal, especially at the beginning of your treatment and any time that your dose is increased or decreased. *(What?!)*

You, your family, or your caregiver should call your doctor right away if you experience any of the following symptoms: new or worsening depression, *(I AM NOT DEPRESSED!)*; thinking about harming or killing yourself *(WHAT??!!)*, or planning or trying to do so; extreme worry; agitation; panic attacks; difficulty falling asleep or staying asleep; aggressive behavior; irritability; acting without thinking; severe restlessness; and frenzied abnormal excitement. Be sure that your family or caregiver knows which symptoms may be serious so they can call the doctor when you are unable to seek treatment on your own.

Your healthcare provider will want to see you often while you are taking trazodone, especially at the beginning of your treatment. Be sure to keep all appointments for office visits with your doctor.

No ... oh no ...I don't want to take this. What? Suicidal?! I would never ... No matter what ... I would never ... but are they saying this would make me feel like I want to do that? WHAT??!

Never, ever, ever, ever did I imagine that one day I would be taking an antidepressant (which I did not know Trazodone was until I read the information sheet). You see, I am 'Miss Positive'! I have spent my career energizing people, lifting people up, inspiring people. I research and share information about healthy brain practices and strategies for living a happy life, including mindfulness, reframing, gratitude, and social connection. I practice these things every day. I CANNOT BE

FUCKING DEPRESSED!

In January 2020, 'the girls' travelled to Puerto Vallarta and spent a week together at an all-inclusive resort. It was so fun! One night, we were having a D&M (deep and meaningful) over wine, and I said, "I've really never been happier than I am right now! I have an incredible family, friends that I love and have tons of laughs with, and work that is really meaningful to me." I meant every word. How, now, can I be anxious and depressed? None of this made any sense to me.

I did know that I needed to sleep. *Ok, I will take these (expletive) pills and then in a couple of weeks I will be better and then I will stop,* I thought.

The prescription information sheet said to take the half tablet one hour before bed. I took the tablet. And I waited.

Before I took the pill, my heart was racing. I felt it increase further within seconds of taking it. I got into bed and picked up my book (the one I had been trying to read for two months and couldn't get through one chapter or remember what I read the night before). My heart rate ramped up further. In no time, it beat so loudly, that I was sure it would explode.

And then the nightmare began.

NIGHT FRIGHT

CHAPTER 6

While in the early stages of sleep, I thrashed and moaned (how do I know that, you might wonder … because I was in and out of wakefulness all night). My heart rate was elevated thoughout. I could 'hear' it pounding. I was having flashbacks to my first husband's suicide. My children's faces flashed across my mind … they looked frightened, they were crying, they were reaching out to me … they were repelled by me … they were afraid of me.

I'd wake up and Randy would say, "Are you ok? What's going on, Deri? You are tossing and turning. Try to breathe. Try to relax."

The poor guy. He had to continue to work under very stressful circumstances. As Executive Vice-President,

Human Resources, he was totally responsible for keeping his organization and all of its employees safe, while also helping them continue to be productive. You see, they couldn't just simply have people working remotely (not that arranging that was 'simple' for any organization). They were an essential service, who provided pharmaceutical technology solutions to hospitals. Engineers and technicians needed to be able to service the product already in the hospitals, and to install new products. And, they needed to travel internationally at a time when most travel had halted or was a general mess. Randy needed to manage all of that, while living with a wife who was not functioning during the day, and who thrashed and moaned all night.

This continued for weeks. Many times, Randy got up with me and took me downstairs. "Let's just try to sit here for awhile. That might help to calm you down so you can go back to sleep." When he held me as we sat on the couch, I seemed to be able to settle a bit. We would head back upstairs and get back into bed. Within minutes, it would all start again.

I saw my doctor for my two-week appointment and told her about my experience with Trazodone. I hated it. I wanted off of it.

"You have to give it time, Deri. These medications generally don't work for at least six weeks."

Are you fucking kidding me? SIX WEEKS?? Geezus! my mind screamed.

"I want to see you in another four weeks," my doctor said. By then, the medication should be working.

Back to the nightmare. And daymare.

DAYMARE FLARE

CHAPTER 7

I woke each day and felt completely shitty. Like a sack of hammers. I had a headache, every part of me hurt, I was hunching over, my ribs poked out, my face was ashen, and my eyes were vacuous. After sitting on the edge of our bed for a minute or two, I got back into bed. And so it went. Day after day. I was in and out of bed. Not sleeping. Just laying there. With my thoughts. Thoughts that I could not track. If you asked me what I was thinking, I couldn't tell you.

Randy checked on me regularly. "How are you doing, Deri? Why don't you come down and have something to eat? Maybe jump in the shower, it will probably feel better. The kids and I are having dinner, why don't you join us. We are taking Bella (Ali's dog) for a walk, do you want to come along?" He was so kind. He was consistently calm and caring. I am sure he wanted to strangle me on several occasions because I not only stayed in bed for most of the day, I kept him awake for most of the night.

One day, Randy said, "You should call Suzanne and Jennifer." (There are two Jennifers in this book … this is my speaker buddy, Jennifer that Randy is referring to.)

I knew I should. I just wanted to be better when I did. I decided to text: *Hi, I am okay, I will be in touch soon.* I wanted to buy some time. *Maybe I will feel better one day, and I will call them then,* I thought.

Well, I did not exactly feel better, but their texts back to me convinced me to agree to a call. They told me how they contacted Ali and then Randy through Facebook. I had not been responding to them and they were worried about me. It took them awhile—a bit of CSI of sorts—because my husband, daughter and son have a different surname than I do. They found a picture on my page in which Ali was tagged, they reached out to her and she put them in touch with Randy.

The video call was wonderful. I did not tell them a lot of detail at the time, but we had a good conversation and I was SO happy to see them. I knew I was very fortunate to have people who cared about me. I wanted to treasure that. (And, yes, my inner critic was alive and well, telling me how I SHOULD do more to appreciate my friends.)

Some days, I forced myself to shower (it often took me over an hour to get in … I would just sit in the bathroom and stare at the shower). Two hours or more later, I would find some clothes to put on and I would head downstairs. Randy would do his usual check in with me, asking how I was doing. "Not good" was my usual response. He'd ask me lots of questions, and although I could not find the words to answer all of them,

I was glad later that he asked because it helped me to kind of 'tune in' to myself.

Some days I had dinner with my family. Some days I went for the Bella walk, although I did not want to be seen (I knew I looked bad having got down to about 104 pounds). Plus, I did not want my neighbours asking how I was doing, I did not want them to know I was taking Trazodone, that I was anxious and apparently depressed. (Even here, in writing this ... I have a hard time with that word, 'depressed'.) I knew they were wondering about me because I often did not return their texts inviting me to join them in a walk and when I did respond, I just said that I did not feel well. In retrospect, I am pretty sure they knew what was up.

The days were agonizingly long. I continued to be unable to focus on anything. I could not read, listen to music, or enjoy a movie or mindless TV show. I tried and tried to be 'normal'. I tried to cook meals.

Many times, Randy would find me just staring in the pantry. Sometimes for an hour. Or, I would go down to the freezer, and keep opening and closing it ... for what seemed like forever. I could not make a decision. Not at all. Sometimes, Randy would suggest something. "Why don't we have pasta and sausage? I'll barbeque the sausage and you make the pasta." I would do it. And I would question myself constantly about whether or not I was doing it right. I could not remember how to make pasta. It frightened me. I did not say anything. I just persevered and did it and I hoped it was edible.

As it got close to the holidays, I was even more antsy. You see, I always loved making the holidays special for the kids—for all of us. I love the decorations, the baking (most of the time I bought it, or Randy's mom provided us with a nice stash of it), the turkey with all of the trimmings, the gifts.

I found myself having a very hard time shopping for the kids. Thankfully, they sent me links to things they liked. They had done that in the past and I had always supplemented that with little surprise gifts as well.

For Christmas of 2020, I could not think of anything else to get them. It really bothered me. Not because the kids would be disappointed or upset (I knew they would not be), but because I somehow saw myself as a failure if I did not do something special for them.

Maybe it was more than that. Maybe it was because I knew that 'the real me' loved to do those extra special things, and I was, deep down, very scared that I had lost 'the real me' forever.

For the last 20 years, we have been getting together with family for Christmas dinner and each of us would bring something to contribute to the meal. Now, with the pandemic restrictions, we were on our own for dinner. I wanted to look at this as an opportunity … no rushing to get dressed and ready to go somewhere or rushing to get the house ready if others were coming here.

Instead, I was just worried. *Do I remember how to cook a turkey? How will I make sure everything is ready at the same time? What if I ruin Christmas dinner?* were thoughts constantly circling in my mind. I still remember the day I bought the turkey. I picked up and put down different turkeys at least ten times. Finally, when I made myself choose one, I started walking to the cash register to pay for it, and then turned around and went back—to look them over one more time.

Agony.

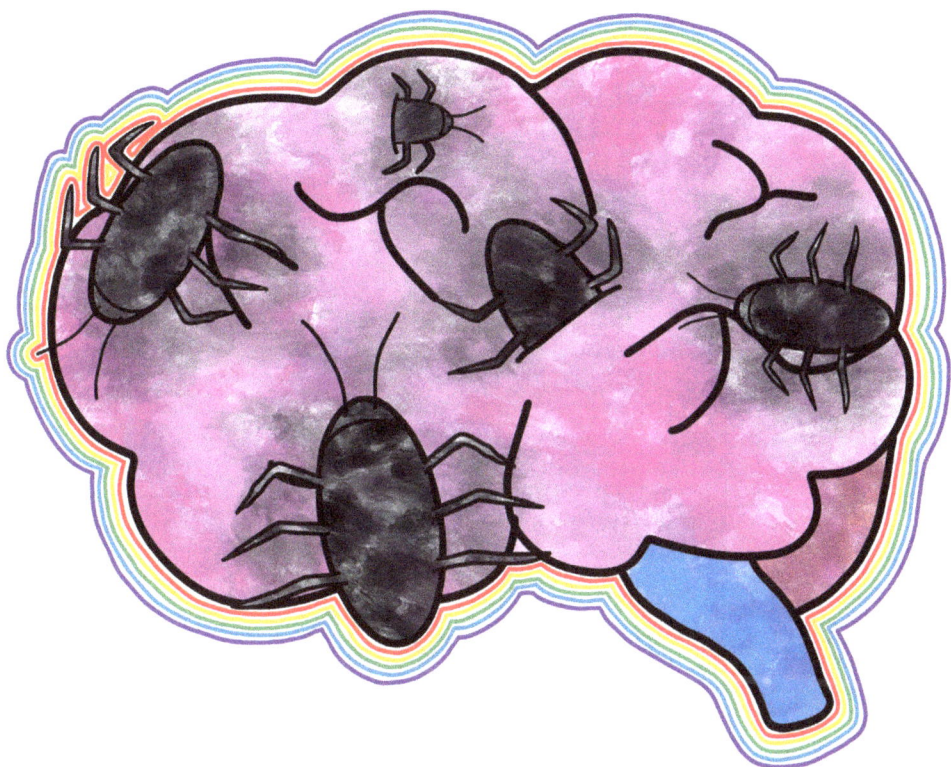

DRUG SLUG

CHAPTER 8

Trazodone scrambled my brain. It simply did not work in any positive way. It was the scariest thing I have ever experienced. I was in a constant state of unrest. Fidgeting, shaking, itching ... Randy said I looked like a drug addict.

One evening, I decided to clean the washer. It bothered me that there appeared to be some mold on the drum. I scrubbed and scrubbed it using all sorts of intense chemicals. In my mind, if I did not get the mold off, my kids would breathe in the spores and they would become sick or die. I scrubbed, scrubbed, scrubbed.

"Randy, look at all of the mold here. This is not good," I said.

"Hasn't it been like that for a long time? I think we are fine," he responded.

"No, it is not good, mold is very dangerous. I saw a show about how a whole family died from mold in their house."

"Deri," Randy said, "it's late. Let me look at it tomorrow. Try to get some sleep."

I couldn't. In fact, I started cleaning the bathrooms because I thought they had mold too. I remember thinking that I was a terrible mother because my house was dirty and we had mold. *What a bad mother.* I could see Randy's irritation growing (certainly can't blame him—I was completely irrational).

The next day, I was still obsessed about the washer and the mold. Our machines were running poorly and the washer leaked from time to time, so finally Randy said, "Okay, I am going to buy some new machines and they won't have any mold."

When the new machines arrived, I somehow believed there was something wrong with them, that they were going to leak water all over and that would cause mold ... and Ali slept in the basement, and the ceiling might fall in on her if the floor in the laundry room got wet. I saw it happening. In my mind. I saw myself running down stairs and trying to pick up pieces of the ceiling to try to find Ali underneath.

Yes, I remember this ... I cannot believe that was me. I am perplexed at my thoughts and my behavior, but I think I can safely say, I was out of my mind.

Now, in retrospect, I can see all sorts of associations between these 'episodes' and some of the messages I got during my childhood about what 'a good mother', 'a good person' should be.

The day the appliances were delivered, our side door was left open for a number of hours. It was a very hot summer and our house seemed to be excruciatingly hot. I went downstairs at one point, and saw a centipede kind of bug on the floor in the living room. Yuk! It was like a big worm with lots of legs and it was black. No one was around. I did not know what to do, but I wanted to get it out. I got a paper towel, and it took me 20 minutes to pick up the bug and throw it outside. Then I ran back upstairs.

And got back into bed.

I had constant, frightening dreams (more like nightmares) as I dozed during the day. In one vivid dream, I was alone at home. Randy, Ali and Max had left me—they were done with me. As I lay in bed, tons of bugs started climbing up the bed—covering me. I was grossed out and scared in the dream but I could not wake up. Later in that same dream, I was outside on the lawn crying. I told the neighbours that my family left me and I was all alone. They just stared at me … like I was crazy.

Oh, yeah … fun times in the Latimer-Howorth household! Trazodone started to kick in with regard to getting some sleep, but I continued to be very restless and I woke up feeling just horrid! A major side effect of trazodone is dry mouth. I sometimes could hardly breath because my mouth was like a desert. Remember those old cowboy movies where the guy was stuck out in the desert for days, and his lips were all crusty?

Well, that was how I felt … and I was still antsy and jittery, and unable to focus or communicate, and had nothing … absolutely nothing … to offer the people I love most in the world. I was constantly uncomfortable. The only small slice of peace I could find was when I got into bed and pulled the covers up and shut my eyes. I would have calm for a few seconds. I guess that is why I kept getting back into bed all day. It was my only slice of quiet.

OVER ROVER

CHAPTER 9

I couldn't wait for most things to be over. I couldn't wait for the pasta-making to be over. I couldn't wait for dinner to be over. I couldn't wait for the day to be over.

Every day I got up, and my first thought was that I couldn't wait for the day to be over.

I saw my doctor after the four weeks. I was sleeping slightly better but I told her I still felt completely awful. Randy came with me to this appointment also. He told her about how I seemed unable to make a decision, that I would stare at the pantry for hours, that I seemed to not want to do much of anything, including connect with people. I remember being a bit irritated with him telling her all of those things. I knew they were true, but I was totally embarrassed.

Why am I acting this way? I asked myself that question over and over. I could not comprehend who and what I had become. It was so lonely. Not only had I disconnected from other people, I had disconnected from myself.

My doctor prescribed Citalopram to take every morning. I did not want another prescription! I spent most of my life being uber-healthy. I hardly take any pills. I hated this!!

The pharmacy information sheet was almost as disturbing as Trazodone.

> **Citalopram, sold under the brand name Celexa among others, is an antidepressant of the selective serotonin reuptake inhibitor (SSRI) class. It is used to treat major depressive disorder, obsessive compulsive disorder, panic disorder, and social phobia. The antidepressant effects may take one to four weeks to occur.**

Geezus! MAJOR DEPRESSIVE DISORDER?

Fuck!

I have a DISORDER now?

Fuck! Fuck! Fuck!

No! No! No!

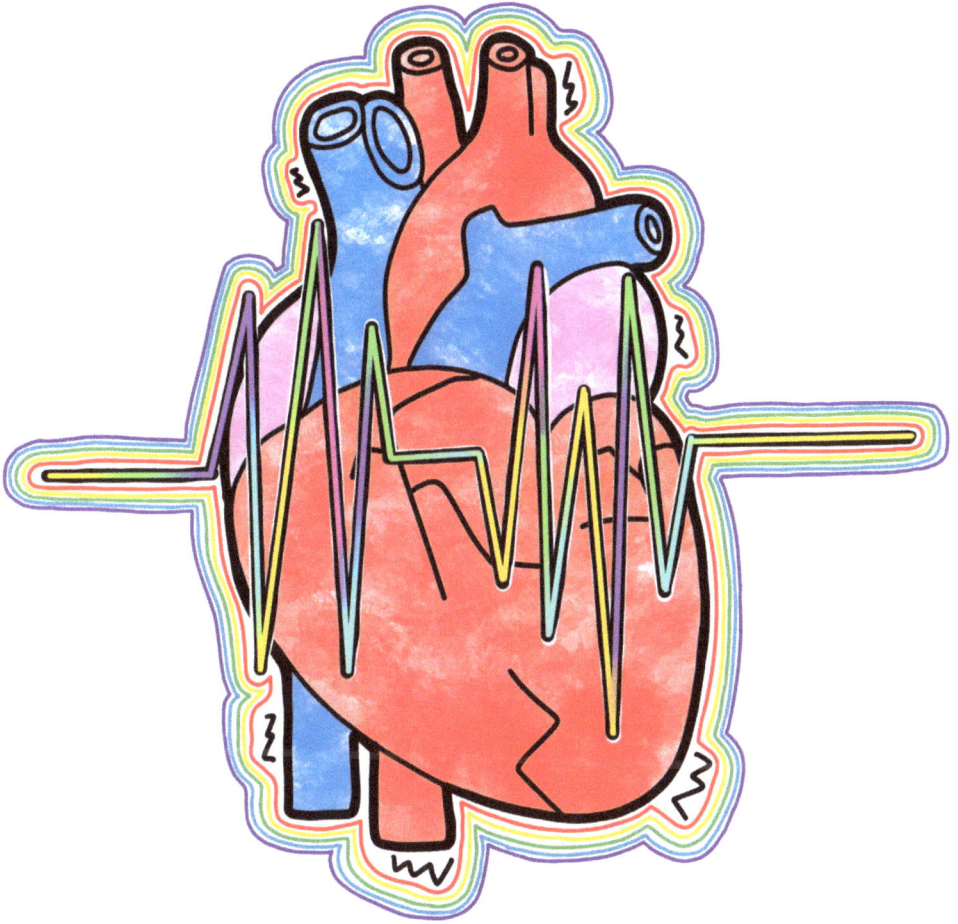

EMERGENCY URGENCY

CHAPTER 10

June 3rd was our daughter's 26th birthday. I was sitting at the computer in my office. Suddenly, I became aware that my left arm ached, tingled and then felt numb. At the same time, my heart rate was elevated, even more than what had become my 'new normal' rapid heart rate. It continued for hours. I looked my symptoms up online.

I think I might be having a heart attack, I thought. I almost welcomed the notion. Then, I can tell everyone that I had a heart attack and that was why I was sick and why I did not return their calls or texts, I rationalized.

I told Randy what I was feeling. I said I wanted to go to emergency at the Victoria Hospital. "Let's wait a bit," he said. "It might just pass."

"Randy, I need to go. Dene died of a heart attack just last year, my dad died of a heart attack at age 45. I could be having a heart attack and I think I should have it checked out."

I am sure I looked desperate.

"Okay, let's go. You know I can't come in with you to wait. And the wait time might be long."

"I know," I said. "I will be okay alone."

We got to emergency at 2 p.m. The waiting room was packed. There was a board on the wall that read: *Wait time 3 hours.*

Fuck, I thought.

Within the first half an hour, I had an EKG. *Excellent,* I thought. *This should go quickly and then I can get home and celebrate Ali's birthday properly because I will be fixed.*

Bloodwork was done in the next half-hour. Randy and I were texting, and I kept him up to date. I remember it was a 35° C (95° F) day and he waited outside for me the whole time, intermittently cooling off in his Jeep, and walking around the parking lot looking for shade.

At 7 p.m., I was finally led into an examination room, all the while thinking, *I am so sorry I decided to come here now ... poor Ali ... it is her birthday and I am sitting here. What is wrong with me? Why did I insist on coming here? I am going to ruin her birthday!* Then I thought, *At least I am in now and should be on my way soon.*

Two young nurses arrived and asked about my symptoms and then hooked me up to some sort of machine—another EKG perhaps? They then told me the doctor would be right in. When

he arrived, I was still hooked up to whatever they hooked me up to. He asked about my symptoms. I told him about Dene, and about my dad. He asked what I was doing when I noticed the symptoms of arm numbness and elevated heart rate. I told him I was just sitting at the computer. He read the screen of the machine to which I was connected, and said, "There are no indications of a heart attack and your blood work and EKG are normal." He asked a few other questions. I could tell in his eyes that he knew I was messed up—that he knew it was anxiety and that I was in a bad way. I could just tell.

I ran out of there (technically, I did not run—but I walked real fast) and jumped into Randy's arms, which surprised us both as I am not a jump-into-my-husband's-arms kind of girl. I just felt so relieved at getting out of there!

"It's all good. It's not a heart attack," I told Randy.

"That's good," Randy said. "Always good to check things out. Let's go home and celebrate Ali's birthday." For a few seconds, I felt what might be called hope. Just for a few seconds.

We arrived home about 7:45 and had dinner—and then cake. I had texted the kids telling them to go ahead and eat without us. I had ordered Chinese food delivery for 5 p.m. and I did not want them waiting since I knew I could be awhile in emergency. But they hadn't listened.

We ate dinner, sang *Happy Birthday*, and followed with cake. Ali opened her gifts and seemed to like everything. (Of course, she did ... she picked it all out.) No extra surprises from Mom. Not this time. It was enough for me to just click and pay.

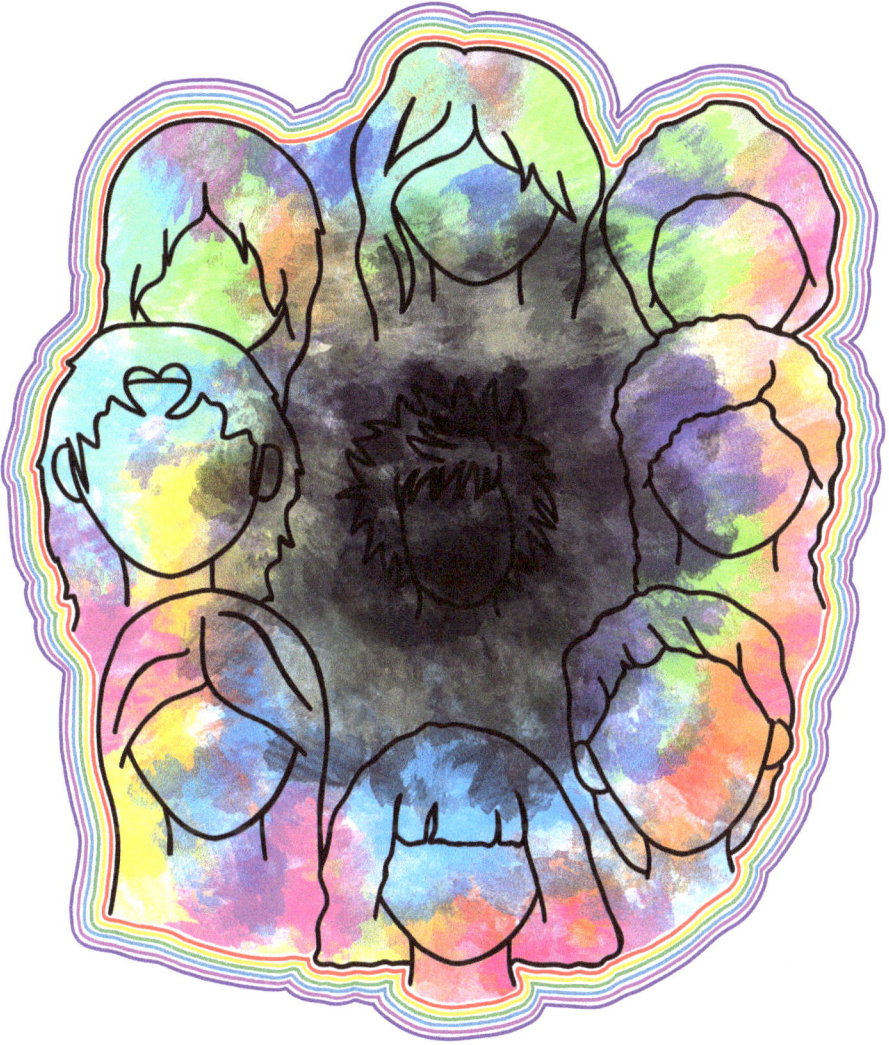

DISCLOSURE EXPOSURE

CHAPTER 11

Eventually the Citalopram started to kick in. (I still felt bad, but at least I could get out of bed and fake that I was completely well.) We asked the kids to join us in the sunroom, that we wanted to talk to them. I had not formally told the kids what was going on for me. Of course, they knew something was wrong, they knew I was not myself, but they did not know the whole story. I had asked Randy to keep it between just the two of us. I did not want them to know. I did not want to scare them or worry them. And I certainly did not want to admit that I needed medication in order to function. I was their strong mom. That's what I wanted them to see, always.

They were so amazing. They listened carefully. I said I was experiencing some elevated anxiety. (I still refused to say the word depression ... still to this day, I do not like that word ...

I think we need a new one.) And, we definitely need a new word for disorder ... seriously, who wants to be disordered?!

When I said that I had been losing weight, I saw Ali nod. "I thought so, Mom ... but I thought maybe you wanted to lose weight because I know you and Dad did a cleanse last year and you said you really liked it. I thought maybe you did that again."

Ali then said, "I understand. Mom, I have anxiety too. I am glad you told us." (That girl has always been so empathic, she helps you to feel that you are not alone—that she's in it with you.) I told them that I was going to do everything I could to overcome this and get back to my old self.

Max said, "We just care about you and want you to feel better, Mom." His eyes met mine and I knew he was with me.

I can cry right now just thinking about that moment. Their faces. Concerned, confused, and caring—all at the same time.

And then a thought appeared—from my inner critic—to mess up the moment. *Deri, look what you are doing to these poor kids, stop it ... just behave normally ... they don't deserve this!*

"Hey, Mom," Ali said. "Can I get your opinion on some of the clothes I got for my birthday? I like them all but am unsure on a few pieces."

"Absolutely," I answered. I can plainly remember thinking, *Wow, she actually wants my opinion ... yay! I guess she has not given up on me yet.* In my 'normal' self, I would never be surprised if she asked my opinion on something. Somehow, now, I was. I was losing complete confidence in myself. I was losing myself.

Father's Day later that month was a disaster. I knew I should do something to make the day special for Randy; I always did. Nothing huge. Just something. Make him breakfast or have a nice family dinner. 2020, I had nothin'.

Randy's sister, Cindy, had already dropped off several meals for us in the past few weeks; for which I was both grateful and simultaneously embarrassed.

On Father's Day, Randy went to visit his mom, and she sent dinner home with him. Again, I was grateful as I had nothing planned and was not sure what we would eat. I was also ashamed. Here was my 90-year-old mother-in-law cooking a huge dinner because her 59-year-old daughter-in-law was incapable of looking after her family.

Groan.

WEIRD REARED

CHAPTER 12

There was weirdness. I had an overwhelming sense—feeling —thought—that I was going to lose everything. I was going to lose Randy, lose the kids, lose my friends, lose it all. This sense grew and grew. I mentioned it to Randy a few times. I did not tell him how overwhelming this sense was.

One night, I woke and just stared at Randy. He opened his eyes and jumped a little. (Pretty strange having someone stare at you as you sleep!)

"Are you guys leaving? You are leaving me, aren't you?" I asked.

"What?" Randy said. "Deri, we aren't leaving you. Where would we go? We are a team, remember. We aren't going anywhere."

"Can you please go check the kids—make sure they are okay?" I asked.

"Deri, they are sleeping. It is two o'clock in the morning. I am not going to wake them up and make sure they are okay. They are okay. Go back to sleep."

"I just have to check," I said. "I will go check."

First, I went into Max's room. He was awake and laying in his bed. I think he likely heard Randy and I talking so he was expecting me. I sat on the end of his bed.

"Oh, hi Max," I said, trying to sound 'normal'. "I just wanted to check and make sure that you are okay. Are you leaving? Is everything okay?"

"I am not leaving, Mom. Yes, everything's good."

"Okay … well that is good. Can you please come downstairs with me to check on Ali and make sure she is okay?" I asked.

"Um … sure, Mom," Max replied.

Down we go, Max following behind me. I enter Ali's bedroom.

"Ali? Hey bud, Ali?"

She awakens, startled. "Huh? Wha..?"

"Oh, hi, it's just me." (No kidding, Deri.) "I just wanted to check and make sure you are okay. Is everything okay? Are you guys leaving?" I asked.

"I was literally just sleeping, Mom. I am not going anywhere," a groggy Ali responded. Even Bella, who popped her head up at

the noise, looked dazed and confused.

I immediately regretted disturbing them. Even though I continued to believe, to think, to sense, that I was losing everything. Earlier that night, I dreamed that they were sneaking out when I went to bed and quietly driving away, leaving me there all alone. I dreamed they went to Cindy and Bill's place. I saw Cindy hugging the kids and saying, "I know I am not your mom, but I will do my best to be your mom." Geez.

For the longest time, I was embarrassed—ashamed—that I actually woke my kids up in the middle of the night and asked them if they were leaving me. No way was I ever, ever, going to tell anyone I did that. That's what a crazy person does. Someone completely off their rocker. Someone who is nuts. *Surely the kids will forget and we won't have to talk about it when I am normal again*, I thought.

There was another day of weirdness. It happened in mid-August, about a month after waking the kids up. I had a COVID test and was instructed to self-isolate for 14 days. I read the sheet they gave me. It said that I need to isolate from everyone, including people in our household. I told Randy and he saw it another way. He thought I just needed to isolate from people outside of our household.

I was fixated on what it said on the sheet they gave me at the testing site. I waited for Ali after she came out of the shower.

"Ali, can you read this please?" I asked.

"Sure, Mom," she replied and she quickly read the sheet. "Okay I read it."

"You see, Ali, it plainly says that I need to isolate from everyone, including all of you. Dad doesn't think I need to do that. But you can see what it says, right?" I asked.

"Mom, I think it is mostly that you need to isolate from other people. I think it is okay," Ali said.

I could feel my body twitching as we talked. I remember at one point; my leg literally flew straight out in front of me. I was wringing my hands. I saw the look on Ali's face and it so saddened me. "I'm sorry, Ali. Did I upset you? Are you okay?" I asked.

She turned to look at me straight on. She had tears in her eyes. "I am okay, Mom. It's just that I love you and that was kind of scary."

I apologized once again. Later that night, Ali decided to go to the cottage to study for a couple of days. I knew she needed a break from the shenanigans at home. We chatted a few times and I checked in to make sure she was okay, and to reassure her that I would be okay.

I am so glad that Ali said that to me ... that what I was doing scared her. It was small moments like that when I was able to snap out of my rumination and back into the present.

I am aware of the stigma around the words 'crazy', 'off their rocker' and 'nuts' being used to describe someone with a mental health concern. But it is exactly what I thought about how I was behaving at the time. I use the word crazy in the title of this book, because I think it aptly describes how I was at that time. A little crazy. And that's okay.

HAIR SCARE

CHAPTER 13

My hair was thinning. After I showered, there was hair everywhere. When I put product in my wet hair, I would look at my hands and they would be covered in hair. It freaked me out.

It was a constant source of anxiety for me. I obsessively searched 'hair thinning women' on google. The pictures and descriptions scared me. *What if I go bald? I can't go bald!*

I mentioned it to Dr. Ahmad at one of my earlier appointments. "It looks just fine to me," she said. Then, she moved on to discuss my medication. She told me later, when I was feeling a little bit better, that she thought that thinning hair was the least of my problems at the time. She was right. I was not sleeping, had lost over 15 pounds, and could not focus well enough to drive myself to my appointments. Little did she know that I was immensely distressed by what I was noticing, in the sink, in the shower, on my hands, on the floor in the kitchen; it was as if parts of me were falling away.

I shared my thinning hair angst with Cindy, and swore her to secrecy (I could not stand the idea of people knowing that my hair was falling out). My hair is not only a significant element in my appearance, as it would be for anyone, it is also my brand. I have had spiky hair with a swirl of bleached blond for more than twenty years. I get many comments on my hair. Some are difficult to interpret, such as "Wow, I would never be THAT brave!" or "Can't miss YOU in a crowd!" Others are clearly complimentary, such as "Great hair" and "I love your hair." I didn't NEED those compliments, but they were very nice to receive. And I really, genuinely liked my hair.

Another friend I told and swore to secrecy, trying to be helpful, said, "If it does all fall out, you will really rock some funky scarves and cool wigs."

I just stared at her. *What?* I thought. *Are you kidding me?*

"I cannot even go there," I told her. And I meant it.

I had no sense of humor about this situation. All I really wanted her to say was that she was sorry that I was experiencing this, and that she believed me. She is a very, very good person and I know she just wanted to be helpful and encouraging. Like most people, she wanted to be supportive —but she wasn't giving me what I needed, or at least not in the way I needed it, to be helpful. This incident reminded me to just empathize when someone is sharing something important to them, rather than trying to solve the problem or say it will be okay, because those responses may not be helpful at all.

I started counting hairs. I know—it sounds crazy! And it was. As my hair continued to shed, I started counting the ones I found in the shower and on my hands after adding product. 35. 27. 31. 64. I counted every day—hoping the number would go down and I could celebrate that it was getting better.

Not only was I losing hair, but my scalp itched and tingled constantly. I mean CONSTANTLY. I searched that online also. I ordered hair products that were recommended for itchy, tingly scalp. Again, the images I found, of women with severe scalp conditions, frightened me.

I brought this up with Dr. Ahmad at every appointment since the first time I noticed the strands swirling around my shower drain. She prescribed a medication to rub into my scalp at night. It did not work. Finally, after realizing that the scalp medication was not working and the shedding was not stopping, she referred me to a specialist, a doctor focused on hair treatment. My appointment was for two months out. I called the office and asked if there was a cancellation list that might get me in sooner and was told that there wasn't but I could phone each day if I wanted to check in.

So, I did. I called the office every morning. After 13 days, I got an appointment for two weeks away. I was so nervous for that appointment. More like excitement mixed with fear (excitement about getting to see him, fear that he would tell me I was going bald!) I was also hopeful. Hopeful that my problem would be solved and my hair restored. Ta-da! Fixed! I had heard that this dermatologist was someone you either loved or hated. Apparently, he could be very abrupt. Even rude. His lack of bedside manner did not scare me, however. I just wanted this problem fixed.

I arrived early for the appointment. The waiting room was full of socially distanced, masked people. Mostly men. But some were women, with quite thin hair. I could not look at them. Inside I was screaming, *Oh, please, please, I cannot be going bald! Please ...*

Finally, I was called in to see the doctor.

"What can I do for you?" he asked.

I told him that I had been experiencing symptoms of anxiety since March and that I started noticing very early on that my hair was thinning and my scalp was itching, burning, and tingling.

He stood up and looked at my scalp. "I don't see anything here," he said. (He literally looked for three seconds.)

I looked back at him. "Well, can you help me? Is there anything you can give me to stop my scalp from burning and itching and my hair from falling out?"

"Listen," he said. "You have nothing to worry about. I see people who have thick crusty scalps and significant hair loss. You have more hair than all of them. You do not have a problem. I can't help you."

And that was it. I waited four weeks for the appointment, 90 minutes in the waiting room, and he talked to me for 30 seconds tops! I left the room, exited the building and got into my car. I just sat there. *Why won't anyone believe me? Why didn't he take my symptoms seriously?* I thought. I felt so very alone. It was a cold, gray winter day and I just wanted to climb back into bed and escape my reality.

When I got home, I called my dermatologist, Dr. Rochelle Van de Velde. I really like her and have seen her for a few years, mostly for random checks of my body for suspicious-looking

marks. Thankfully, I have had very few things that caused her concern, and I always feel better after seeing her.

I was able to get an appointment for three weeks out. Amazing. She is very busy and usually the wait is months long, but I just happened to call when there was a cancellation that needed filling.

In the meantime, I ordered shampoos (six different kinds), vitamins (I read that biotin was good for hair growth), lotions and potions that advertised they could help with thinning hair. I did not think it was strange that I had 12 bottles of shampoo or conditioner lined up in the shower. My husband commented on it once, asking if I used all of them.

I replied, "Yes, I want them there, I need them there so I can try them and see what works." He looked at my determined face and decided not to mess with me and my shampoo. He never mentioned it again. The row of bottles is no longer in our shower. (Instead of berating myself for buying all of that stuff, I neatly put them away and know that I am now set in the shampoo/conditioner department for at least five years!)

I showed up early (even though I could not go in early, thanks to COVID protocol) and waited in my car. I counted the minutes, staring at the clock until it was time to go in. The reception room wait was relatively short, and then I was escorted to an examining room. While I waited for Dr. Van de Velde to arrive, I whispered to myself, *Please, please, please Dr. Van de Velde ... please help me.*

She walked into the room and was her usual perky, pleasant self. "What can I do for you?" she asked.

I repeated my problem to her—the itching, burning, tingling, shedding story. She listened carefully and asked all sorts of questions, "When did you first notice this? Is the itching and burning all over your head or just in certain areas? Did something happen around the same time as you started to notice this?" All the while, she typed into her computer. She was genuinely listening to me, her voice and entire demeanor communicated that she cared about me, she heard me—she BELIEVED me!

Once she collected the initial information, she stood up and checked my scalp thoroughly. "I am not seeing anything worrisome here. Your scalp looks healthy." Then she turned to me, took out a piece of paper and a pen, and she proceeded to tell me what she thought was happening.

"This looks like a condition called telogen effluvium." She explained that telogen effluvium is the name for a common cause of temporary hair loss due to the excessive shedding of resting or telogen hair after some shock to the system. In March, I had a significant shock to my system.

"With this condition," she said, "new hair continues to grow. I see some new hair coming in on your scalp." I wanted to hug her, to marry her, to lick her face. She drew pictures of the various stages of hair growth and thoroughly explained telogen effluvium. She 'normalized' what I was experiencing.

"I experienced this after each of my pregnancies," she said. Then, I remembered that after Ali was born, I would find my long hair wrapped around her little fingers. I remembered that I had some hair shedding then too. It was after Ali's birth and my experience losing some of my hair, combined with being a new mom who wanted an easier hairstyle, that I first got a short, spiky hair cut. I loved it and have not looked back since!

Dr. Ahmad and I talked about every two weeks. Each time, I was honest with her. "I still mostly feel like crap. I don't want to

socialize, although I make myself. I don't want to make meals, although I make myself. I have absolutely no energy. No pep."

Seven months into this nightmare, she said, "This is taking too long, Deri. You should be feeling better by now." She took time to check with a psychiatrist on my behalf; she wanted to be sure she was not missing anything by way of addressing my symptoms. After that, she decided to change my daytime medication to Venlafaxine.

Great, I thought. *First, I have to wean off the Citalopram, then start the Venlafaxine and wait another six weeks for it to start working. If it does at all.*

I continued to feel miserable, but in a few weeks, I did note an ever so slight change in how I felt. I still felt atrocious, but maybe 1% less atrocious.

It was winter in Winnipeg. It was a particularly gray winter— or maybe that was just my perspective. Thanks to COVID restrictions, all we could do was walk. I yanked my ass outside every day to go for a walk. It took everything in me to go. I NEVER wanted to go—I just made myself. I could not wait for the walk to be over so I could go back home and hide.

I would listen to my friends talk as we walked. They shared recipe ideas, movie ideas. I had nothing to share. I listened. I nodded. I said the odd "that sounds delicious" or "really?" But I could not have given a rat's patootie about any of it. I tried really hard to fake enthusiasm and normalcy. Every time I drove to meet the girls for our walk, I was secretly hoping they would call and cancel.

Every time.

MESS DISTRESS

CHAPTER 14

I became very messy. I left clothes out in piles on my dresser and even on the floor. I left my hair products and makeup out rather than putting them away after I used them, which I had always done before.

I did not clean. At all.

Finally, Randy asked, "How about I do the bathrooms and the vacuuming, and you do the dusting and the sweeping?" I thought that made sense. (Even though my brain was still not working well, I did realize that Randy likely had no idea how much work it is to clean our bathrooms, two of which have large showers.)

He did do what he said he would do.

I didn't.

At least not very often.

My office was complete chaos. I left EVERYTHING out. Every day I entered that space, I thought to myself that I really do have to sort things out and clear some space. But I didn't. It seemed that I couldn't. *I'll do it tomorrow—for sure,* I said at least 100 times to myself.

I was actually happy that we could not have any people over, because I would be mortified if anyone saw the mess I was allowing in our home.

As I reflect back now, I think my space was reflecting what was going on in my mind. My mind was, indeed, messy. Chaotic. I suppose that is why my space became so as well.

THERAPY CLARITY

CHAPTER 15

I knew I wanted and needed to go to therapy. I went once when I first started feeling poorly, early in May.

I called a psychologist who is rather well-known in Winnipeg. I inquired about whether I might be able to get in to see him, fully expecting it to be weeks out (or months). Certainly, we were already hearing about more and more people in some kind of COVID crisis.

"How about tomorrow at 2:00?" the receptionist said.

"Great," I said.

I showed up early and waited in my car. Suddenly I wasn't sure I wanted to go in. I told myself, *You need to go. You will feel better. You don't want to keep feeling like a piece of shit, do you?*

The office was VERY quiet. I was the only one in the waiting room. There was a sign instructing visitors to remove their shoes and wait to be called in. The receptionist did not even acknowledge me; I sat there and stared at a vase on the table.

A couple came into the office. I occupied my mind briefly with imagining their story. They seemed uncomfortable with each other, there was a strong energy between them. I guessed that they were divorced or divorcing and that they were there for couples counselling (a specialty service of this particular therapy office).

Finally, an office door opened and the psychologist looked at me and said, "Deri?"

"Yes," I said, standing up and following him in. The office was beautiful and spacious. We sat across a small table. He asked the 'What can I do for you?' question and I told him what was going on. This was early on (40 days) in my journey of feeling like a piece of dung—before medication, before the hair shedding and before the waking the kids up in the middle of the night.

"Well, I just don't feel good. I am generally a very positive, happy person. In fact, I am a professional speaker and 'positivity' is my brand. Organizations hire me to inform and inspire others, encouraging them to practice simple strategies for resilience and brain health. Right now, I know I cannot inform, inspire or encourage anyone. I am in desperate need of all of that myself. I just feel really 'off'—not myself. I am not sleeping. I am hoping you can help me to sleep.

"What else, besides wanting to sleep better, are you looking

for from this therapy?" he asked.

"I want some hope. I want to know that I will be okay and will feel better soon."

He asked questions that led me to share some of my story, including Kelly's suicide. "I really think I have dealt with that," I said. "It is not like it is on my mind all the time. In fact, I have even shared parts of it from the stage during some of my keynote presentations. And, in 2013, I delivered a TEDx talk in which I shared the story through the lens of the night I told my children. I really think I have done the work I need to do around that traumatic time in my life."

He asked a few more questions and I shared how my mom had passed away in October of 2018 followed just five months later by my older brother, Dene in March of 2019. While Mom's death was somewhat expected, Dene's was a complete shock. "These are 'fresher' wounds, of course, but I really think I am dealing with that grief. I have always been a 'deal with it and move on' kind of person. And, that is what I have done."

I talked most of the appointment, as is expected with therapy, and especially in the first session where we were just getting to know each other and he was in the information-gathering phase.

"You seem to be able to compartmentalize well, and what I hear you saying is that strategy has worked for you so far. Think of it this way, an emergency room surgeon, who suddenly sees that the critically injured person before her is her daughter, has to compartmentalize her emotions around that and focus on using her skills to save the life before her," he explained.

"Compartmentalizing can be very useful 'in the moment' when you need to focus your attention in a specific way. When we compartmentalize as a habit, or for an extended period of time, the impact can be overwhelming. The 'reality' of the stressful event is not processed."

At this point I was only partially following what he meant. On the surface, I understood; but I could not see what this had to do with my not being able to sleep.

"I work a lot with soldiers experiencing PTSD, or Post-Traumatic Stress Disorder," he said. "They are able to compartmentalize the thoughts and feelings of their reality at war, from the skills they need to use to get themselves and their fellow soldiers home safely. They look perfectly in control. Then, when they return, the real trauma surfaces."

"There are all sorts of options we can use to help them process the trauma," he continued. "Sometimes, we have the soldiers watch scenes of people dying in war. We are there with them, but it is important for them to visit that place again in order to really heal it. For you, I might show you pictures of people who have died by suicide."

WHAT?! Show me pictures of suicides?! What?! Are you fucking kidding me? I thought.

I could not focus on anything else that he said. I honestly felt like something in my brain 'snapped'. I just stared ahead and nodded until my appointment time was up.

I could hardly wait to get out of that office.

I never went back.

The next day, I went for a walk with Cindy. I told her I felt like shit. Randy knew I was not feeling well, but no one else did at this time. "Maybe I have anxiety or something; my heart is beating out of my chest, and my head hurts. I have no energy. No 'oomph.'" I explained.

In addition to being my friend, Cindy is highly empathic and caring. She is also a social worker, so I thought it might help to talk to her and get her perspective on what might be going on with me. I told her about my experience with the photo-showing psychologist, and how horrified I was that he might show me pictures of suicides. I also told her that I was finding it very hard to focus on anything, to even search out other therapists.

After our walk, within twenty minutes, Cindy sent me three names. That's the kind of gal she is. She researched psychologists, checked them out on an MD rating website and sent me her best three recommendations. Thank goodness. I hadn't been able to do it myself, my brain was too foggy, but she helped me move forward by taking on the research.

It took me over a week to make the first call to book an appointment. I have no explanation for why I did not call right away. I simply couldn't.

Finally, I dialed the number of the first psychologist on the list. We played telephone tag. She did not have a receptionist, and handled booking all of her appointments herself. I, as you now know, was notoriously not in the vicinity of my phone.

So, I would call and leave a message. Then, a few days later, she would call and leave me a message. Then, a few days later, I would call and leave a message, and so on. This went on for weeks.

Finally, we connected at the end of July. She said she was booking into September, so we agreed on two appointment dates. I would have booked an appointment for every day if I could have; I just wanted to get well.

She sent me a bunch of paperwork. One document asked for the usual information—name, address, etc. Another asked my reason for why I was coming for therapy, how I would describe my relationships with my parents, and other similar questions.

Several pages were filled with lists of various conditions that I was to rate myself from 'Never' to 'Every Day'. Questions like "Do you believe that you deserve this?" or" Do you have thoughts of harming yourself?" Most things I rated very low, choosing the 'Almost Never' option. I was definitely not suicidal or experiencing thoughts of harming myself, nor I did not believe I deserved what I was experiencing or that others were out to get me.

When the first appointment came, I sat in my car waiting to go in five minutes ahead of the scheduled time. At EXACTLY the appointment time, she arrived to escort me to her office. (I will admit, it irritated me. My appointment was at 10:00 a.m. She walked out to get me at exactly 10:00 a.m. Not even 9:59 a.m. Then, we still have to walk to her office … 'on my dime'.)

When she opened the door to the office, she said, "I hope you like dogs."

Wha…? Isn't that something you should clear with people BEFORE they come to the appointment? I thought, sarcastically. Everything irritated me.

I actually love dogs, but have a bit of a fear of large dogs due to an unfortunate childhood bite. Luckily, the dog was a teeny tiny beauty with a bow in her hair. She sniffed me once and

never paid attention to me again.

The first appointment was agony. I cried through most of it. I was feeling so crappy. Just like a pile of steaming excrement. The psychologist seemed very nice, but I certainly did not feel any better when I left that appointment. I had another one scheduled for two weeks later. "Is there any chance I can see you more regularly?" I asked. She told me she was completely booked. (COVID was keeping psychologists very busy!) I was so motivated to get better, I told her, that I would come any time if she could let me know when she has a cancellation. She said she would let me know when/if that occurred. It never did.

Every two weeks for almost three months, I saw her. I felt like crap when I got there and like crap when I left. She was lovely, but here is an example of how our sessions went:

Me: I feel like I am losing everything, my family, my friends.

Her: Oh, you aren't losing everything, Deri. Your family and friends love you. (Imagine this in a bit of a sing song-y, almost patronizing tone.)

What did I want? I wanted her to probe. I wanted her to say, "Tell me what's going on when you think you are losing everything?" That is what I wanted. I did not need someone telling me that my family loved me. I did not need someone figuratively patting me on the head and saying everything will be okay. Before each of the last few appointments, I rehearsed how I was going to tell her that this was not working, that I appreciated her help, but that I need to try something else

During my last appointment, I said, "I do not feel any better. I don't think this is working."

She agreed. "I believe you have some unresolved grief, Deri. You've been through a lot. You might want to try EMDR. I don't really know what it is, but have heard good things. I know Dr. Kelly Penner Hutton is booked solid years in advance, but—if you want—I could call her and ask her if she would see you. Would you like that?"

"Yes, please," I said.

I went home and looked up EMDR. Again, I could not really concentrate to read about it, and—to be frank—I did not really care what it was. I'd try just about anything at this point.

I called Peace of Mind Therapy and Consultation and asked if I could see Dr. Penner Hutton. I was told that she was fully booked. I then told the receptionist that my previous therapist called Dr. Penner Hutton to ask if she could get me in as a favor. It took a few days and several calls, but eventually I had an appointment with 'Dr. Kelly', as they call her, for four weeks out.

More itching, burning, scratching, shedding, body aches, upset stomach, and overall weightiness and crappiness. There was not one second from the time I opened my eyes until I got into bed that I felt anywhere even remotely good.

I told my brother, who was a wonderful support to me all the way through, "I get up every day waiting for the day to end so I can go to bed." I find that even tough to type right now. But it is the truth.

One day, my friend Jennifer sent me a message that profoundly affected me. I had been very unresponsive with everyone. However, in spite of this indifference, she continued to send me messages, texts, voice mail hello's—for months!

Messages like this one:

> *You are in the midst of a difficult time and that just makes you human, most certainly no less wonderful than you have always been. I want you to know that it makes no difference to me if you are feeling up or down, I love you just the way you are. I'm just going to keep sending you stupid little things to let you know I'm thinking of you—'cause I am, a lot! Everyday!*
>
> *Don't feel like you need to be anything other than who you are in this moment. Seriously, if you just want to take time to heal, that's cool. You don't need to reply. I expect nothing from you until you're ready.*
>
> *Don't feel like you need to be all together and happy, either. I'd be honored to sit quietly with you and just listen to the wind, if that felt like the right thing. Totally no expectations and no judgement.*
>
> *Meanwhile you're stuck with me* 😉

And this one:

Hello my friend,

I feel that I wasn't very helpful yesterday. As you may or may not realize I've lived with anxiety and depression for most of my life. For me, it's pretty normal so I've learned to coexist with it. I get this is not your normal, so not helpful for me to think I have a true understanding of how frightening it must be to feel these things as a new experience.

What I do think is you are having a reasonable response to a challenging couple of years. I've seen you bravely navigate your mother's death and the shock of losing your brother. Both of those things are a heartbreaker.

You have also shown me your beautiful, generous heart. You consistently respond to the people you love in the most open-hearted and welcoming way. The way you supported Dene over the last several years, during very difficult times, was incredible. You provided him with a safe, non-judgemental space to join, on his own terms. I've seen you do the same for your children, even when every fibre of your being wanted to fix their lives.

You've talked about maintaining mental health all these years. You've changed lives, Deri. Don't question your expertise or understanding, just because you are human. You've been through challenges most people can't even imagine. You bring your special gift of light and wisdom to

each group.

You matter. I just want you to know I see you. You are a beautiful soul and I'm so grateful to have you as a friend. I'm sorry you are suffering right now and I wish I could take it away. Hopefully I can offer you a safe, non-judgemental space. No pressure, but I will keep checking in with a hello!

Love you!

And then …. THIS ONE:

Honestly Deri, there was a time when I had been feeling that I wished I was dead—and know when I say that it's different than being suicidal. I have no intention to harm myself, more that I just don't see any purpose or value in dragging myself through all this shit. When I look ahead, I don't see much to look forward to—my parents will die, I have no children to watch live their lives, and my siblings are all older than me so I probably get to watch them die too. Are you more depressed yet? Anyway, being totally honest about how deep the depression goes for me at points and as I said, this is not a new feeling for me. I've sometimes gone months in a state of complete anxiety and self-criticism and depression—like DEEP. There is a way out, I promise.

You're in a terrible place right now, my friend. If I could change it for you, I would. You can trust me, even though I know nothing. Wait! I know a few things for sure. You're made of the very best stuff—a woman of light, love and joy. You'll find her again, she just needs a little time to feel the pain of the world and awaken her next purpose. Just breath. That first breath is the one and then the next ...

Love your healing sister

I stared at the first line. I knew what she meant. I did not want to admit it to myself, and I DEFINITELY did not tell anyone else. But I felt the same—many times. I wanted to be dead. I was exhausted and overwhelmed at feeling so bad for so long. I was tired, really, really tired. Simultaneously, I could not find one moment of peace, of rest.

I also knew I was not suicidal. I had no thoughts of ever wanting to harm myself. I can say for sure that I would NEVER do that to my family. Never. I just wanted to not be where I was.

My healing sister. We started calling ourselves that a number of years ago. Our conversations were always so rich, and we have similar interests in well being, meditation, mindfulness and all things healthy. We share our celebrations and our frustrations. We listen to each other. We help each other. She is, indeed, one of the most intelligent, caring, creative, calm and energizing people I have had the pleasure to call a friend— and a healing sister.

Finally, the day arrived for my appointment with Dr. Kelly. Again, I felt like a shit-covered sack of bones. As I sat in my car in the parking lot, I told myself to be hopeful. When I arrived in her office, she gave me some paperwork to complete. The

same paperwork I completed for the last psychologist. When it was time to go into her private office, she asked if I am okay with dogs (what's up with therapists and dogs?).

She was training a therapy dog, Sarah. Sarah was a big dog, young, with a playful energy to her. I was mostly disinterested in her and just wanted Dr. Kelly to keep her away from me. (In time, I actually grew to enjoy seeing Sarah; coincidentally that was only once I started to feel better.)

Our first session was a get-to-know-you session. Dr. Kelly said we would start processing in the next session. EMDR or Eye Movement Desensitization and Reprocessing is a form of psychotherapy developed by Francine Shapiro starting in 1988. During the process, the person being treated is asked to recall distressing images; the therapist then directs the patient in one type of bilateral stimulation, such as side-to-side rapid eye movement or hand tapping. According to the 2013 World Health Organization practice guideline: "This therapy is based on the idea that negative thoughts, feelings and behaviors are the result of unprocessed memories. The treatment involves standardized procedures that include focusing simultaneously on (a) spontaneous associations of traumatic images, thoughts, emotions and bodily sensations and (b) bilateral stimulation that is most commonly in the form of repeated eye movements."

I liked Dr. Kelly. She seemed like a no-nonsense kind of gal. I also liked that EMDR was something I could 'do' ... rather than just talking (which I did not enjoy or find effective). It is interesting, when you watch a talk therapy session portrayed in a movie, the therapist asks really amazing questions, and can quickly connect the dots for the client. Not so much for me so far. Meeting Dr. Kelly gave me renewed hope.

After sharing some new coping strategies I could use to

manage my uneasiness, we began working through my memory network.

Dr. K: What is the worst symptom you are experiencing now?

Me: Lack of motivation.

Dr. K: When was the last time you felt like this?

Me: Yesterday

Dr. K: What image represents the worst part of it now?

Me: People are frustrated with me, yet I cannot seem to do anything about it.

Dr. K: What words go best with that image that expresses your negative believe about yourself now?

Me: I am out of control, I am helpless.

Dr. K: As you think about yesterday, what emotions do you notice now?

Me: Fear, sadness, lack of confidence.

Dr. K: Where do you feel that in your body?"

Me: In my chest and head.

That questioning approach continued in my appointments, as Dr. Kelly and I explored my memory network. I remember Dr. Kelly asking me again about the 'worst part' of what I was experiencing, and I answered 'losing my self-confidence'.

Dr. K: When was the last time you remember feeling that you

lost your self-confidence?

Me: When Kelly died. (Yes, my first husband's name was the same as my therapist—that was never weird though.)

Dr. K: What's the earliest memory you have of feeling that you lost your confidence?

Me: I am about six or seven years old. I am with my older sister and her friend, at her friend's house. Her friend's mom was a good friend of our mom. We girls were on the second floor playing barbies, when we somehow ended up in the mother's bathroom. We started looking at her makeup and admired all of the colours and textures. I particularly loved the lipstick. One of the other girls put some on me. I thought I looked beautiful.

A while later when we got home, our mom was livid. Apparently, the other mother called her and told her we got into the makeup. My mom blew a gasket. "How could you? I am ashamed and embarrassed! I thought I raised two young ladies but clearly I did not." (By the way, this is in no way parent-bashing. My mom was a lovely, incredible human. She, like all humans, lost her noodle from time to time.)

Dr. K: What is the strongest image of the worst part of that time now?

Me: We are in the bathroom. I don't know where my sister is; I just see me and my mom. I am looking up at her, crying hysterically and saying, "Please Mom, I love you, I am sorry, please Mom, don't be mad."

And then my mom said, "You can't love me if you would do something like that! You don't love me!"

Dr. K: What words go best with that image/memory that

expresses your negative belief about yourself now?

Me: I believe that I am a bad person. I believe that I am responsible for my mom being upset. I believe that my mom does not think I love her, and maybe she doesn't love me either.

Then, we started processing the memory. I cannot describe it all to you ... I was completely 'in' it and cannot recall each and every step. Dr. Kelly would guide me through the image, the experience of that memory; we stopped regularly to 'process' with eye movement and hand-held paddles (which buzzed in synchrony with the lights).

After processing, Dr. Kelly asked me to take a deep breath, and then—on a scale of one to seven —rate how distressing the image was for me in that moment. We would keep processing until I was comfortably at a one or zero.

Then, I remember this:

Dr. K: When you bring up that image now, what would you like to believe about yourself now?

Me: That I am human. I make mistakes. I am a good person. My mom knows I love her and she loves me.

More eye movement with lights and paddles.

Dr. K: Bring up the image and the negative belief about you being responsible for upsetting your mom, what emotions do you notice now?

Me: I am sad, I am scared.

Dr. K: Where do you feel that in your body now?

Me: Chest and head. Maybe a bit in my gut.

Some of the themes that arose during processing included:

- Mom and I never talked about what happened that day.
- Mom is human too, she just got hijacked/triggered that day.
- The little me felt scared and rejected, which led to self-judgment and criticism.
- I want to tell little Deri that it is okay to make mistakes.
- I want to hug little me (embracing rather than rejecting).
- I need to keep sending good messages to myself: "It is okay to make mistakes", "I'm just human."

As we did more processing on that memory, the image that represents the memory changed. I could see myself hugging my mom and telling her that it's okay, because she would have felt very bad for how she reacted. Finally, I felt good with that memory and my emotions were those of calm and acceptance.

As we moved through the memory network, Dr. Kelly could determine that some of the other memories that arose around the 'lack of self-confidence' theme were not as strong or bothersome to me. We moved through those and then on to the most distressing memory in the network, Kelly's suicide.

Dr. K: As you bring up that memory, what image represents the worst part of it now?

Me: Getting the phone call about him being found.

Dr. K: What words go best with that image/memory that express your negative belief about yourself now?

Me: I am to blame.

Dr. K: When you bring up that image, what would you like to believe about yourself now?

Me: I am human. It is not my fault.

Dr. K: Bring up the image and the negative belief, 'I am to blame'. What emotions do you notice now?

Me: Horror, guilt, shame.

Dr. K: On a scale of 0-10, where 0 is neutral or no disturbance or distress and 10 is the most you can imagine, how disturbing does it feel to you now?

Me: Not sure, a low number, I think. (This was likely avoidance coming out as a protective measure on my part, but I am not sure.)

Dr. K: Where do you feel it in your body now?

Me: Gut, chest, head.

Themes that arose during processing, in order, were:

- I don't enjoy visiting this memory, I have worked hard to reframe it.
- I feel anger; many body sensations in my gut and chest.
- I am starting to breath better, feel lighter.
- I am not feeling blame, guilt or shame.
- I am starting to feel distance from the memory.
- The pandemic left me feeling very out of control.
- Conflict is difficult for me, and when I am around people who are angry or in conflict with me, my self-confidence and motivation are affected.
- I would like to work on that part of myself, to not be afraid of conflict, to know it is normal.

- As we moved along and checked in on the scale of 0-10, I answered with 5-6.
- I am starting to notice the discomfort I had avoided.

Dr. Kelly ended every session by sharing a new coping strategy I could use to take care of myself between appointments.

We continued processing Kelly's death.

Dr. K: What image do you have of the exact moment you heard about Kelly's death?

Me: I am sitting on the couch. There are people there but I cannot hear them. I am numb.

Dr. K: What emotions are present now?

Me: Fear, shock, shame.

Dr. K: Where is that in your body now?

Me: Head, chest, shoulders—very heavy.

Over the next few sessions, what I was experiencing started to shift.

Dr. K: What are you noticing now?

Me: I feel bad for myself (this was a new perspective that emerged). I feel kindness and compassion for myself.

I started to notice that the memory seemed farther away. I

felt calmer and more accepting of myself when I brought the memory to the surface.

I started to respond with compassion for myself and for Kelly. I am human. And so was he.

With each question Dr. Kelly asked, I just said the first thing that came to my mind. It was remarkable to me that I could answer any question she asked.

And so, the weeks went. We processed the memory of Kelly's death very deeply over the next ten sessions that were held every two weeks.

A couple of days after session six, I woke up and knew instantly that something was different. I did not feel like a sack of hammers covered in excrement. I felt—dare I say—good.

I worked out (*omg, I still feel good*), showered (*yup, still good*), went shopping, came home, made dinner—and at each moment checking in and thinking, *Wow, I still feel good!*.

I did not say anything to anyone. I was worried it would not last. I wanted to see what happened.

The next day, when I opened my eyes, I knew that the shit covered sack of hammers was back. Dang.

After session eight, I woke and felt really good. It lasted all day. I told Randy. I almost whispered it. "I feel really good, Randy. I have not felt this way in over 14 months."

"That's great," he said. He was likely skeptical, as was I, that it would last. Randy has been with me every step of the way through this ordeal. The man deserves a medal. If I did not already love him to bits, the way he handled this situation only enhanced my feelings for him. He is one. good. human.

The next day, I said the same thing to Randy. "I feel really good!" And the next. And the next.

When I saw Dr. Kelly for my ninth and tenth sessions, it became clear to us both that I was done with the memory of Kelly's death. It had been fully processed.

Of course, Kelly's suicide was awful. It will always be awful. But what has changed is that it is no longer distressing to me. It can be awful and not distressing.

When Dr. Kelly asked me for the last time what image comes to mind when I go back to the memory of hearing about Kelly's death, the only image was that of Kelly's face. He looks peaceful. He looks gentle. He looks kind. Exactly as I remember him being when he was alive.

We had one more session just to see if there was anything else I wanted to process around every day irritations. I told Dr. Kelly that I am just happy to be alive and to feel good. No irritations.

Now, that does not mean that I will never have irritations again, of course. What it does mean is that I am going to apply all that I have learned about what I need to do to be well, so I am ready for irritations, trauma, joy and ecstasy!

Right now, I am embracing the joy!

NOT CRAZY, *Just Human*

CRUSH RUSH

CHAPTER 16

I have a bit of a crush on Gabor Mate. I first encountered the retired physician and author when he came to speak at our children's middle school in 2005. I was on the parent council at the time and was asked to introduce him. He was discussing his book, *"Hold On To Your Kids: Why Parents Need to Matter More Than Peers."* It was a compelling read and reminded me of the important role we parents play in our children's lives. It can be particularly challenging during the teen years, when our children sometimes seem uninterested in being around us and certainly in listening to us.

I am sure you can only imagine what I put my poor kids through. Being a prolific reader of positive psychology and well-being, I constantly shared what I had learned with them—over dinner, on a drive, wherever I could squeeze it in. They often kidded me about how often I said, "Evidence shows ...." I could not resist sharing what research told us about how to life a good life; strategies like:

- 🌸 reframing negative situations more positively so you can open up more options for moving forward;
- 🌸 pausing and reflecting regularly, during which you can remind yourself that there is no right and wrong in your communication with others, there is only 'different' ... different perspectives, assumptions, interpretations; and those interpretations are not 'reality', they are a story we make up about reality; and
- 🌸 listening to the 'voice in your head', the one that is constantly nattering at you, and realizing that the voice is often negative towards you, but it might come with a purpose to protect you in some way ... and although you can change the voice in your head to a more positive loving one, you can also appreciate that the critical one might just be there to help keep you safe.

(If you have already tuned me out reading that, just imagine what it was like being my child!)

One day, when Ali had friends over, I overheard her speaking. She sounded just like me! She was saying many of the things I had shared with her. *She actually listened,* I thought, smiling inside.

Any parent knows 'that look' from a teenager that seems to say, "I know, I know ... you have said that a thousand times. Leave me alone!" Dr. Gabor's book showed me that I needed to matter to my kids, and I definitely did not want to "leave them alone." It is a challenge, though, isn't it?

I was always so grateful that I had friends like Cindy, with whom I could have authentic conversations about raising

children. It is easy to think that you are constantly messing up!

Looking at Ali and Max today, I see two incredibly lovely human beings of whom I am immensely proud. Did I mess up along the way? For sure! Will I continue to mess up? Absolutely! And, I will continue to stay close to them as they move into their independent lives. (Don't worry, Ali and Max, I won't be calling you five times a day to check in on how you are doing or to tell you the newest on what "evidence shows"! Or, to wake you up in the middle of the night.)

In 2019, I attended a three-day workshop with Dr. Mate on Compassionate Inquiry. I had been studying Mindful Self-Compassion for years, and I thought this might be a great learning experience for me. My friend, Jennifer, told me about it; it was advertised mostly to health care professionals, so I felt so lucky to be able to get a ticket to attend.

I was completely mesmerized. I remember telling friends that I felt like I was levitating off my chair as I listened and watched him as he worked with people on stage. Everything he said made sense to me. Since then, I have become a frequent follower and watcher of his YouTube videos, and the new movie about his work, 'The Wisdom of Trauma'.

I KNOW that I was ill for fourteen months because I had a trauma that was triggered in March of 2020, with a phone call from a friend informing me of the recent suicide of her son. The anxiety was simply a symptom of what was going on underneath (the trauma, and the beliefs and feelings associated with that trauma). This is exactly what Dr. Mate's life work is all about. This is why I have a crush. I literally believe that his work HAS and WILL save lives.

My life's work is to use my voice to share information that might be helpful for people to live a good life. I am privileged to find myself on platforms around the globe, and I want to use my voice to share not just my story, but what I have learned from people like Dr. Mate, with anyone who will listen.

Below is a collection of quotes (many are not direct quotes but are a reflection of what I heard) from Dr. Mate that I love. In *italics and yellow highlighted* are the quotes as I remember them from Dr. Mate. In brackets and non-italicized, I explain just a little about what that means to me and possibly for you.

There are two kinds of people, those who have had trauma and know they have had trauma, and those who have had trauma and don't know they have had trauma.

(As I have shared some of my story of the last 14 months, I can see it in people's eyes and I have heard it from their mouths ... something like "Oh, you have had trauma, Deri. Not me, I had a good life. I have not had trauma." What I have learned is that we all have trauma. Trauma does not have to mean that you were raped or tortured or violated in some way. It can be something as simple as your mother losing her shit because you made a mistake, and you—unknowingly—told yourself that you had to be mistake-free or you might not be loved.)

Trauma is not what happens to you, it is what happens inside of you as a result of what happens to you.

(I have thought about the memory I shared in THERAPY CLARITY, of my mom being so upset at my sister and I for embarrassing her. It all makes sense to me now. My mom, like everyone of us, had trauma. Mom did not talk a lot about her life growing up, at least she didn't when I was younger. Later,

when I was an adult, she shared some stories. Mom was the oldest of two girls, born to Peter and Mary Procyshyn. Both had minimal education, I believe Mom said that she thought Grandma had not made it past Grade 2. Peter, my grandfather, was 16 years older than Mary, my grandmother. The way Mom remembered it, Grandpa sort of 'made a deal' with Grandma's father to be able to wed Grandma. Their relationship was a volatile one. Grandpa had a serious drinking problem.

Mom said that when she was eleven or twelve, Grandma would send her off to the Legion Hall Pub to get Grandpa to come home for dinner. One particular day, as Mom headed off to the Legion to collect her dad, she found him passed out in the middle of the road. Pretty embarrassing.

Years later, when Mom was twenty years old, she landed a job as the secretary to the Mine Manager. (Sherritt Gordon Mines was the main employer in Lynn Lake.) Grandpa worked as the custodian in the mine at the time. One day, months into her employment, Mom's boss called her into his office and told her that her dad has been caught stealing money from someone's pocket in the change room and he was going to be fired. Pretty embarrassing.

So, is it any wonder that years later when her two daughters do something that embarrasses her, that she completely loses her noodle on them? Nope. I think not. I think that is completely expected. Mom's trauma was triggered by our behavior on that day, and she was completely unable to do anything but what she did.)

Parents can be so stressed that they do not see their children, engage with their children or empathize with their children as much as they would otherwise. (This is not parent-bashing, it is just stating what is happening.) When children are not seen for who they are, they make one of two assumptions: 1) my

135

parents are not capable or do not love me, or 2) something is wrong with me. For the child, it is safer to assume #2, that there is something wrong with them, because for a four-year-old to endure the assumption that their parents aren't capable or do not love them is untenable. They cannot live with that. So they choose the other assumption.

(Remember in THERAPY CLARITY when I talked about Dr. Kelly's questioning process of my six-year-old memory with my mom; this is exactly what happened in my six-year-old brain. I thought there must be something wrong with me. This happened unconsciously, and affected the belief and then the coping strategy I chose from that day forward—be 'good' and you will be loved.)

When someone treats that child compassionately, the child thinks 'okay, maybe I am a worthwhile human being.

(I believe this is such an important point. Most of us as parents are not schooled in compassion, we are not taught how to be compassionate with our children, or with ourselves. If we can help parents learn how to be compassionate, maybe … just maybe … we can prevent a future addict or suicide victim or human who finds themself feeling like a sack of shit at age 59 and not knowing what the fuck is going on!)

We are born with certain expectations from the world. We have lungs and our lungs are there with the expectations of oxygen, otherwise we would not have lungs. Our nervous systems are developed with the expectation of love, of being held, enjoyed, nurtured. Whether the child develops well or not depends on how well those expectations are met. We can survive without them, but we cannot thrive without them. We can adapt to their absence, but we are not thriving. Much of disease (physically and mentally) arises out of the ways we had to adapt where our natural expectations were thwarted.

(Just sit and read that over again. Then stop and think about it. We all adapt. Something happens, and we adapt. Often, those adaptations are not healthy—such as abusing substances, suppressing emotion, over-exercising, over-eating—and over time, we become ill. I encourage you to read Dr. Mate's book *"When the Body Says No: The Cost of Hidden Stress"*. Mind blowing.)

The negative voice in your head is not a given. It is just a reflection of society. That is what civilization has done to humans. Kids are not being valued for who they are, and they install a voice to keep themselves in line. It is a natural adaptation to challenging circumstances. In this society, it is tough for parents to deliver <u>unconditional positive regard (Carl Rogers)</u> because they are under so much stress. Parents under stress put the child under stress. This happens even in utero. Then, 50 years later, that child (now adult) is diagnosed with a disease. That adaptation gets wired in and then becomes a problem later on.

(When I shared my summation of this with a friend recently, she said, "That sounds like I am to blame for having cancer." Clearly, that is not what Dr. Mate says, or what I believe to be true. This is not about blame. This is about understanding. My mom is not responsible for the adaptation I chose from that early experience. She is not to blame. Kelly is not to blame for my illness over the last 14 months. There is no blame. There is only understanding.)

We are wondering why kids have mental health and behavioral problems, yet we focus as a society on medications to correct behavior. Instead, we should be asking "Why is the child developing this way?" We need to spend far more time on emotional well-being than on language skills and scholastic achievement.

(I have always believed this ... for as long as I can remember ... certainly since I became a parent. Let's educate children in understanding their brains. In developing healthy beliefs about themselves. In learning coping strategies that work FOR them rather than AGAINST them.)

My work in palliative care is so fulfilling. I can listen and get to know people without pretending. I am not pretending and neither are they if they want to die right. In my book, "When The Body Says NO," I tell a story of a gentleman who sold shark cartilage as a cure for cancer. There was no scientific basis to it, but he believed it. Then he got cancer. He ate it until the end. I remember visiting him, and as soon as I stepped off the elevator, I could smell the shark cartilage. It smelled horrible. I asked him, "How does it taste?" "Terrible," he said. "Why do you keep eating it," I asked. "Because my business partner would be so disappointed if I did not." He kept eating the cartilage until he only had days left to live. How different could it have been if he stopped pretending earlier and spent his remaining time on other things.

(I love this story. I can think of people I know who are behaving in ways that are hurting them. They are choosing to stay stuck with limiting beliefs about themselves and about others. They are being hurt. And they are hurting others. I wonder what it would be like for them to choose to let go of those limiting beliefs and learn another way to be in the world. I think it would be wonderful.)

Any deep pain you experience, you are confusing the present with the past. When you are triggered, you can focus on the trigger (what someone said to you, for example) or you can focus on the ammunition (past trauma).

(My friend calling me about her son's suicide was the trigger. The ammunition was my past trauma.)

Present suffering is a measure of past suffering—conscious and unconscious memories. What you are experiencing now is a measure of the past, and you can learn to reinterpret it now.

(Almost every keynote I have delivered in 25+ years includes the power of 'telling yourself another story', of reinterpreting situations in a way that can be more useful and productive for you. I've known this for years and have a kajillion examples to share with audiences. Learning about EMDR and marrying that with the work that Dr. Mate is doing, has convinced me that the ONLY reason I got well was because I had the opportunity to have a professional (Dr. Kelly) take me back to process those past memories and to change the voice in my head about those memories AND because I have discovered Dr. Mate's work on trauma, which only solidifies what I know to be true about the last 14 months of my life.)

Use Compassionate Inquiry when you are triggered. 'I reacted that way ... why did I react that way?' asked with curiosity (not, 'WHY DID I REACT THAT WAY?', with judgement). Then use compassion to look at yourself. 'If I reacted that way, there must be a good reason for that.' Rather than putting yourself down, you have curiosity to explore and compassion to not judge.

(Talk to yourself like you would talk to someone you love. Yes, the voice in your head comes with a tone. Remind yourself that your reaction carries a message; a moment of learning for you. In my 2013 TEDx talk, in which I shared the story of the night I told Ali and Max about Kelly's suicide, I ended with three C's representing what Ali and Max taught me that night. "Be Curious, Caring and Connected," I said, "with others and with yourself.")

The common template for all affliction is, in fact, trauma.

(Yes, you read that right. I interpret this as 'All of what ails us as humans, comes from unprocessed trauma. If we only treat the symptom ... anxiety, for example ... we cannot cure the source, and it will surely rise up again.)

*There is wisdom in trauma. **We can work through our trauma and become ourselves.***

(People have said to me, since I got well in mid-May of 2021, "You seem different ... almost too happy, too assertive." Some people have even called me aggressive. There is some truth in that. I am different. I feel different. I see the world differently. I interpret things differently. It is a VERY GOOD kind of different, for me. I speak my mind more freely.

I know now that I lived most of my life being 'nice'. I like to be nice, and I do not look back on my life and believe that I was 'faking it'. I just never learned to speak up, especially when I disagreed with another person, or if I was disturbed by what they had said. I learned to just 'be good, be nice, and be liked'. Now, I am not as much interested in being liked as I am interested in being heard, respected, valued. That is different for people who have known me in another way.

I respect and value others, and will continue to ensure my communication is respectful. I am sure I will mess up from time to time; I will say something stupid or will overreact because I am triggered by something that someone else says.

At my core, is a value of caring for others. People who really know me know that. Never do I intend to do or say anything to cause another person to be in pain. I might, though. Because I do not know what their triggers are. I only hope we can talk about our relationship and how we impact each other—both good and bad—and that we can own our own stuff along the way as we continue to learn and grow every day.

I spent 14 months in a state of 'freeze'. Unable to look after myself. Unable to think. Unable to DO anything. Now, I live in a state of freedom and action.)

Underneath your trauma is a healthy person.

(Dr. Mate's work with addicts is transformative. An addicted person is a traumatized person. And, underneath that trauma is a healthy person. I think that message is one this world needs right now more than ever.)

Lastly, this one, which is so cool:

On my epitaph, on my headstone, I want it to say, "It was a lot more work than I anticipated."

I love that! Thank you, Gabor!

Life is work. Being well is work. It's worth it!

Through the teachings of Dr. Mate, I know that I can be okay with the word *depression* (even though I still think there is a better one because there is so much stigma associated with it). I know now that the reason it was such a loaded term for me during this ordeal, is that Kelly likely experienced depression. And, he died by suicide. And, suddenly I felt like a truckload of manure. And, the medication I was on was called an anti-depressant. And, I did not want what happened to Kelly to happen to me.

I wrote a blog in June, called 'Hangin' with Harry: The Brain-Changing Beauty of EMDR (you can still find it on my website:

https://www.derilatimer.com/blog/). I had just watched Prince Harry talk about EMDR on "The Me You Can't See" collaboration he has with Oprah. I am so pleased that EMDR is getting that kind of international coverage and good press. It worked for me and I'd love it if others knew more about it also.

Harry also shared that we need a new word for PTSD (Post Traumatic Stress Disorder). He suggests the term PTSI (Post Traumatic Stress Injury) is more appropriate, and might help with the perception of it and encourage more people to seek help. As Harry put it, "You have experienced an injury, you are NOT disordered." I like that. I was injured (temporary), I am not disordered (permanent). When I describe myself to others, as we talk about what I went through during the pandemic year, I do not say I had anxiety or I had depression, I say, "I had a trauma that was triggered and it took nine months before I got the help I needed through EMDR."

That, to me, is the truth.

WORD STIRRED

CHAPTER 17

One evening in June, I drove to Ali's place and went for a walk with her and Bella. On the walk I told her "I am good, Ali. Really good. I feel fantastic, normal ... maybe even better than normal."

I saw her face light up and her eyes sparkle, "Oh, Mom, that is awesome. You seem really good." And then we continued our walk.

A few days later, I got this text from Ali:

> *I've been meaning to say this since we went for our walk because I don't think I articulated it properly while we were walking, but I am so incredibly proud of you and how you've handled*

this whole situation. Watching you not give up and fight for your health honestly has given me so much hope for the future. Just because something shitty happens doesn't mean that that has to define the rest of your life. You were the strongest woman I have ever met before all of this happened but now there's absolutely no debate! ❤ ❤ ❤

My heart felt so full. I responded with:

Oh, my Ali ... I will save this message forever! Thank you SO much for these amazing words. You made my day ... my year ... my life!! I am so grateful for the incredibly articulate, gracious, kind, caring, creative, beautiful (I could add another thousand words) human you are! And, thank you for all of the love and support you showed me – even when I woke you up in the middle of the night!

Throughout her life, Ali has written me notes or texts, in which she shares how she feels. Many are like this one. A spontaneous burst of love. Max has a different style. While he may not write a note or send a text like Ali, he will say a few words that are packed with meaning. "Good for you, Mom" from Max is loaded with love and pride.

A few years ago, Ali's gift to me at Christmas was a notebook called 'Notes to My Mother'. Inside were notes from her to me under different categories, such as *'My favorite memory of us travelling together is ...', 'I am most like you when...', and 'You taught me...'* I got choked up when I opened it. Then I decided that I would read one note a month for the next year. It was so fun opening a new note every month. I totally looked forward to it!

The next year, I decided to write Ali and Max one note per month. I left Max's in his office (Ali's old bedroom that we made into Max's study space) and I mailed Ali's to her at her apartment.

Ali often thanked me for the note or made a comment about something she thought was funny in the note. Max said nothing. That was okay. I had no expectation that they both would or should experience the monthly note the same way.

One day, I was dusting in Max's office, and I noticed all of my notes, neatly stacked on a shelf. It was clear that they had been read. I believe they meant a lot to Max, too. He just has a different, quieter way of being in the world.

I respect and value them both for who they are.

LEARN CHURN

CHAPTER 18

So, it is over. This is over. I am healed. For now.

I am off all medication. I feel healthy and strong. And my brain is on fire (in a good way).

395 days. 9,480 hours. 568,800 minutes. 34,128,000 seconds.

Every experience is an opportunity for learning. I am in the business of sharing what I have learned with others.

Here is what I have learned through this experience, that might help you too:

Balance Your Interests And Those Of Others

Early on in life, I started to believe that I was responsible for other people's feelings. So, I made sure that I was kind and caring toward others, that I did not do anything to upset other people, and that I always put the interests of others ahead of my own. I don't recommend this for anyone. This past year, I realized that we can balance our own interests alongside others and still be respectful, empathic, compassionate and caring to ourselves and to others. I recommend you do the same.

Separate Actions From Intentions

I learned to believe, as a young child, that love could be given and taken away, based on my actions. My mom definitely did not intend to foster this believe in me; she was the most kind and caring human I have ever known. However, during my growing up years, my mom was stressed. If we did something that embarrassed her, her only means of communicating to us how much she cared about it, was through her withdrawal of love. Mom never, actually, withdrew her love, but for a six-year-old girl who desperately loved her mother, hearing, "You can't love me if you did that" was like cutting me with a knife. I made sure to never, ever do anything that might cause my mom to question my love for her. I became an obedient, loving daughter who was no problem for her mother. That was my role.

Give Negative Emotions Space

I have a hard time with difficult, what we might call 'negative', emotions. Anger, grief, frustration … these are challenging for me. Generally, I have adopted a 'Just move past this … don't make a bid deal of it … focus on something positive, approach'.

While that can be helpful at times, it is not a good practice to have as one's usual approach, as one's habit. Dr. Kelly helped me to learn how to sit with negative emotions; to recognize them when they are there, be curious about them, identify where they are in my body, and give them space. To 'be' with them, knowing that there is a message underneath them, before moving on to a strategy to move beyond them.

Take Time To Smell The Rock

I learned to smell the rock. Literally. One of the first exercises Dr. Kelly had me do was a sensing exercise. Pick up a stone and describe the stone. When I first picked up the stone in her office, I said, "This is a stone, it is small and it is black." That was it. After some prompting by Dr. Kelly, I could add, "It has a rough texture with small smooth pieces placed sporadically. It is heavy for its size. It smells like the potpourri bowl in which it sat." I could have added the sense of taste, but I stopped short of licking her rock.

In my Mindful Self-Compassion Short Course that just ended a few weeks ago, we did an exercise on mindful eating. It was remarkable to experience taking time to look at the food you are about to eat. To gaze at the texture, the size and the shape of it. To imagine all of the hands that had to be involved in getting that food onto your plate. To smell it. To let it sit in your mouth before gobbling it down. I hope I will eat mindfully more often. It increases the pleasure ten-fold.

Recognize How And When You Are Triggered

'What happened' in March of 2020 is the following:

1. I was experiencing some fear and confusion at the news of a global pandemic.

2. I went into isolation for two weeks, with my husband who had to work non-stop helping his organization deal with the impacts of the pandemic on their business and the livelihood of their staff.

3. Our daughter experienced a very upsetting situation at her school. I did not know how to help her. I tried to console her as best I could, but it really—physically—made me feel sick. As a mother, I wanted to 'make it all better' for her. I couldn't do that and I felt like a complete loser.

4. A colleague called to tell me about her son's suicide.

All of these happened within days of each other. Since I really wasn't talking to too many people at the time, I ruminated and shoved down whatever I was feeling because it was distressing to me. This set of emotions, thoughts and behaviors mirrored the ones I had in 1988 when Kelly died. Experiencing them all together in such a short period of time, triggered me, sending me back to that unresolved grief, confusion and fear, and sense of loss. Loss of Kelly and loss of myself.

Feel Better Then Figure It Out

Initially, it does not matter why something is happening, you want to relieve the pain and then can make space to inquire. I tried—once I could focus a little—to watch videos about anxiety, wellbeing, and healing. One day, I watched a clip of Eckhart Tolle with a small group of people—it was a Q&A format. From his website, he is described as "widely recognized as one of the most inspiring and visionary spiritual teachers in the world today. He has introduced millions to the joy and freedom of living life in the present moment. Eckhart's profound, yet simple teachings have helped countless people around the globe experience a state of vibrantly alive inner peace in their daily lives. His teachings focus on the significance

and power of Presence, the awakened state of consciousness, which transcends ego and discursive thinking. Eckhart sees this awakening as the essential next step in human evolution."

In the video clip I watched, someone in the audience asked, "My head seems to be constantly filled with thoughts. They can be disturbing and interrupt my day or affect my mood. Where do these thoughts come from?"

Eckhart sat silent for a while, and then said, "If you were suddenly shot with an arrow, would you spend time wondering who shot the arrow, or why they shot the arrow, or would you just want to get the arrow out? Clearly, you would just want to get the arrow out. It is the same with distressing thoughts. It does not matter where they come from in the moment, you just want to do something to end your suffering."

I may not remember it exactly as he said it, but it went something like that. I thought about that a lot through my ordeal. Understanding why is not your priority. Your priority is to feel better. Then you can work on understanding why.

I resisted taking medication. I took it but resisted it. What I now know is that I NEEDED medication—I needed relief—in order for me to be able to process and heal.

Write Positive Messages To Yourself

I still find notebooks around my office and in my bedside table in which I wrote positive messages to myself, like:

- You got this!
- You can do this!
- It is going to be ok
- You will get over this!!!!
- BELIEVE

155

- Choose
- Do it, even if you don't want to!
- You are loved
- Your family believes in you
- Your friends care about you
- YOU GOT THIS!

Those notes made a difference. I wrote them almost every day. Some days I didn't believe them, but I wrote them anyway.

Before this happened, I would regularly write down what I was grateful for. This is a common happiness practice recommended by both scholars and practitioners. When I reflect back, while I was isolating at the cottage, where all of the craziness began … I did not keep up this practice.

When we forget or neglect to do what we know is a good practice, our brains use that space for other things. In my case, my brain went to ruminating and worrying. Once I started to feel even a little bit better, I started my gratitude practice again. It matters. Do those things you know you need to do— every day. You brush your teeth every day. You need to do these things too.

Practice Presence

Every one of us needs to spend time practicing presence— every day. I had a regular meditation practice before all of this, but I did not continue it regularly while we were isolating. I was consumed with reading about what was going on in the world, with worrying about my kids, with wondering what the future would be like. When I started to get sick, I couldn't meditate. I tried. I simply could not be still. I could not focus on my breath.

When the medication kicked in, and my brain began to be more balanced, I was able to meditate again. Although it was very difficult at first, (I was still feeling quite horrid and had not achieved the clarity and comfort I eventually got from EMDR), I made myself 'sit' each day. I made myself be quiet. I made myself focus on my breath. Even if I could only focus on one breath.

Jon Kabat-Zinn, known as the father of mindfulness, titled one of his books 'Wherever You Go, There You Are'. I reminded myself of those words several times through this ordeal.

Celebrate Successes

I praised myself. I know, because I have studied and spoken on the topic of resilience and happiness for over 20 years, that it is critical to focus on the positive—to focus on what is working, not on what is broken. So, I would take a minute or two each day to celebrate my accomplishments—with myself! At first, it was, "You had a shower today, Deri. That is good." And, "You had a great conversation with Max. Way to go!" Or, "You were more engaged and interested on your walk yesterday with the neighbors. You go, girl!"

Yes, sometimes it felt strange to be talking to myself, boosting myself up, but I did it anyway. And it made a difference.

It is so easy, I think, to beat ourselves up for what we haven't done, for what we wish we had done, for what we did that we wish we hadn't. We can get very lost in that negativity. Of course, we all need to know if we do something and someone else is hurt by that. We need to make amends. However, we need to spend at least ten times the amount of time and effort celebrating what is right with ourselves, with others, with all of humanity.

Cut Yourself Some Slack

One day last summer, I went for lunch with my brother, Devin. I am so grateful that we have always been very close. (Other than when he was young and annoying, of course!)

While we ate our Thai food during lunch, Devin shared about a time ten years ago when he went through a tough situation.

"You were there for me, Der. You were always there for me. I want you to know that I am here for you too." That was good to

hear. He continued, "One day, when things were getting better for me, we were out for coffee, and I started talking about the tough situation again. I remember you saying, 'Oh, I wondered when that might come up again.'"

"Did I really say that," I asked. "Like in a 'mean' way?"

"Yes," Devin said. "It was as though you just wanted to talk about something else—about something good, and you did not want to keep talking about that same bad situation. I am only telling you this because it might be affecting you now ... if you are being impatient with yourself, if you are judging yourself, if you are trying to just get over this, it could be damaging you."

I thought about that a lot when I got home. Thanks, Dev. That was a huge gift to me. Even though I do not remember saying that a decade ago (and really do not ever want to be that way with others who are sharing something with me), it was a good reminder that if I don't want to be that way with them, I should not be that way with myself.

Remember Your Goodness

People are good. This has always been a belief that I have held. Throughout my entire career—first in Human Resources and later as a conference keynote speaker and consultant—I have always believed that people are essentially good at their core. When they do not behave 'good', it is usually because something is missing in their lives. This belief has always helped me to be more empathic and compassionate toward others. I reminded myself of that belief many times. I wanted to believe that others had the belief too and that they would have empathy and compassion for me when I was behaving unlike myself. It is a good belief. If you do not already have it, I recommend you adopt it. Life is much easier.

If you are fortunate, your friends will remind you who you are. I remember early on during the pandemic, my friend Cindy said to me, "Remember who you are, Deri." I did not really understand what she meant then, but I do now. Remember your core beliefs and values—remind yourself of them every day—because when you are sick, it is very difficult to access them.

Suzanne and Jennifer (speaker buddy Jennifer) planned a surprise on my 60th birthday in December of 2020. They arranged, with the rest of our Mastermind group (Meg, Peri, and Cate) to surprise me with a zoom call. They sang *Happy Birthday* and they said really nice things about when they first met me. I cried through the whole call. I had no words. It was really beautiful and I felt unworthy of all of that love.

After the call, Suzanne sent me a gift. In it was a heart-shaped word cloud with all of the words that they each said about me—adjectives to describe me. She also included a jar filled with heart shapes with one word on each heart, and a set of metal balloons with string attached that I could fasten to the wall. "Take one word out of the jar each day and put it on the string. Look at the word and remember who you are and what you mean to people," Suzanne wrote. I couldn't do it right away. I kept looking at it every day, but could not seem to read the words and display them.

Five months later, I did it. Those balloons with strings and beautiful heart shaped papers with those adjectives hang in my studio in our home. I look at them every day to remind myself of who I am.

Remember your goodness. Remember that you matter. Writing that note, making that call, sending that text, might be just the lifeline that person in your life needs to hang onto that day. Roxy, my gym instructor, regularly sent me texts or emails

with just a line or two, 'DERI! I MISS YOUR FACE!!' or 'DERI, WHERE ARE YOU!!' Roxy is bigger than life, and her capital letters reflect her voice tone!! I only recently got to tell her just how much those short messages meant to me. I was losing myself. Those messages brought me back to my life. Back to myself.

If you are a doctor, remember how much your clients depend on you. I was fortunate to have a family doctor who listened to me, who asked me questions, who was curious about my therapy, who shared her own strategies for well-being. I always felt heard and cared about. Dr. Ahmad taking time to listen and inquire, had a significant impact on my eventual recovery.

Make Friends With Your Emotions

There will be more bumps, blips and blunders. At the time of this writing, I feel completely fantastic! Like I could run outside and hug the FedEx driver, like I could dance in the rain (it is actually raining right now as I write this). It will not last. And that is okay. When you feel fantastic, embrace it, feel it, love it—be there. And when you feel sad, frustrated, angry, worried—be there too.

One of the most important strategies I learned from Dr. Kelly was to 'be' with negative emotions. To sit with them. Notice where emotions are in your body. Breathe into them and allow them space to be there. Then, after you do that, move toward some action that is meaningful to you and that allows you to move through that emotional state. And always remind yourself that the emotion is there to help you in some way. (I know I already said this, but it bears repeating.)

In one of my keynotes on resilience, I share brain research about what happens when you experience negative emotions.

If you suppress the emotion, it just gets bigger in your brain. When you have a habit of shoving your emotions down, one day, they will erupt. Also, if you ruminate on, focus on, and talk endlessly about the emotion, you reinforce it in your brain and body, and it just gets 'bigger'.

So, first identify it (sometimes I even say, "Hello, anxiety ... I feel you ... I know you are here to help me.") Then notice where it is in your body and give it some space to 'be'.

Lastly, make it your friend, because that is really what it is. This mechanism was developed through human evolution to keep us safe. Trust that those emotions are there to work FOR you, not AGAINST you. Make friends with them.

Be Fiercely Compassionate With Yourself

The learning continues. I listened to Dr Rick Hanson and Forrest Hanson's *Being Well* Podcast in July of 2021. It featured an interview with Kristin Neff about her new book, *Fierce Self-Compassion*. I had the complete honor of experiencing Dr. Neff in Winnipeg, where she led a group of mostly health care professionals through her Mindful Self-Compassion approach. I heard about it because of my healing sister, Jennifer, who is now a prominent figure in the Mindful Self-Compassion movement in Winnipeg.

During the interview, Dr. Neff explained that fierce self-compassion is different than the way she defined self-compassion in her early work. That definition was about kind, soft, gentle self-compassion. Now, Dr. Neff has discovered, that we need 'fierce' self-compassion too, a stronger, bolder, more assertive self-compassion. As I listened, I realized that a part of what made me sick was that I had anger toward Kelly for what he did. I was mad that he chose to die rather than be with me. That he chose to leave me.

Until that moment listening to Dr. Neff, I never allowed myself to admit that I was angry with him all these years. Instead, I had told myself that was a 'bad' way to be, *How dare I be angry with him; he is dead, for goodness' sake.* But if I were fiercely self-compassionate, I would be able to say to myself, *Dang right I am mad at him and I have every right to be!*

I plan to be more fiercely self-compassionate in the future.

CONCLUSION
RESOLUTION

I am Good.

I am Human.

I am energized and re-focused on the important work I care about, for which I am passionate.

I am eternally grateful for my family and friends who kept me anchored in the present and kept believing in me (and helping me believe in myself).

Not crazy, just human (maybe a little crazy).

Resources OfCourses

BOO WHO

Deri Latimer Choose Life https://youtu.be/_mie1tkHbqE

PANDEMIC PANIC

Willard Reaves https://en.wikipedia.org/wiki/Willard_Reaves

ISOLATION SITUATION

Mossa On Demand http://mossaondemand.net

Canadian Association of Professional Speakers https://www.canadianspeakers.org/

SLEEP CREEP

Canadian Family Physician: Zopiclone https://www.cfp.ca/content/53/12/2124

Trazodone https://www.webmd.com/drugs/2/drug-11188/trazodone-oral/details

DAYMARE FLARE

Compassion Matters https://www.psychologytoday.com/ca/blog/compassion-matters/201305/4-ways-overcome-your-inner-critic

OVER ROVER

Citalopram https://www.webmd.com/drugs/2/drug-1701/citalopram-oral/details

DISCLOSURE EXPOSURE

Inner Critic https://www.goodtherapy.org/blog/psychpedia/inner-critic

THERAPY CLARITY

Prince Harry EMDR https://www.wptv.com/news/health/prince-harry-sheds-light-on-emdr-therapy-for-trauma-and-anxiety

Peace of Mind Therapy and Consultation https://peaceofmindemdr.ca/

CRUSH RUSH

Dr. Gabor Mate https://drgabormate.com/

Dr. Gabor Mate, Hold On To Your Kids https://drgabormate.com/book/hold-on-to-your-kids/

Compassionate Inquiry https://compassionateinquiry.com/

Dr. Garbor Mate, When The Body Says No https://drgabormate.com/book/when-the-body-says-no/

Unconditional Positive Regard https://www.verywellmind.com/what-is-unconditional-positive-regard-2796005

Hangin with Harry https://www.derilatimer.com/hangin-with-harry-the-brain-changing-beauty-of-emdr/

Prince Harry https://en.wikipedia.org/wiki/Prince_Harry,_Duke_of_Sussex

The Me You Can't See https://tv.apple.com/ca/show/the-me-you-cant-see/umc.cmc.4amwght1qtt8ioilwr0mgnf6d?ctx_brand=tvs.sbd.4000&itscg=MC_20000&itsct=atvp_brand_omd&l=en&mttn3pid=Google%20AdWords&mttnagencyid=a5e&mttncc=CA&mttnsiteid=143238&mttnsubad=OCA2019901_1-526312078241-c&mttnsubkw=122664159316__RsflbJSa_&mttnsubplmnt=

Oprah Winfrey https://en.wikipedia.org/wiki/Oprah_Winfrey

Psychiatry.org: PTSD https://www.psychiatry.org/patients-families/ptsd/what-is-ptsd#:~:text=Posttraumatic%20stress%20disorder%20(PTSD)%20is,sexual%20violence%20or%20serious%20injury.

The Recovery Village: PTSD vs PTSI https://www.therecoveryvillage.com/mental-health/ptsd/related/ptsd-vs-ptsi/

LEARN CHURN

Giving Thanks Can Make You Happier https://www.health.harvard.edu/healthbeat/giving-thanks-can-make-you-happier

Eckhart Tolle https://eckharttolle.com/

Mindfulness https://www.mindfulnesscds.com/

Rick Hanson https://www.rickhanson.net/being-well-podcast/

Self-Compassion https://self-compassion.org/

Fierce Self-Compassion https://self-compassion.org/fierce-self-compassion/

Center for Mindful Self Compassion https://centerformsc.org/

Compassion Action https://compassionaction.ca

GRATITUDE ATTITUDE

I am eternally grateful to my health care providers:

Dr. Suffia Ahmad, Family Physician
Dr. Rochelle Van de Velde, Dermatologist
Dr. Kelly Penner-Hutton, Psychologist EMDR

For the respect and care you provided to me, and for helping me to continue believing that I would recover.

FAMILY SHMAMILY

I am most grateful for this incredible group of humans
(and one canine) who are my heart, my joy, my life.
Thank you for hangin' in with me!! I love you!

Deri Latimer, BMgt(HR), CSP

Everything Deri does, every decision she makes, and every interaction she engages in or initiates has at its very core the purpose of continuing to create a better world for her children and any other people who might ultimately become part of her family!

Deri is an expert in positive possibilities for people! Turning personal tragedy into purposeful action, she transforms research in neuroscience, positive psychology, and human performance to deliver a message that is loaded with simplicity and practical application. A TEDx Speaker, author, and organizational consultant, Deri combines a business degree with over 20 years of experience engaging audiences across every sector. One of fewer than 17% of speakers globally who hold the designation of CSP (Certified Speaking Professional), Deri inspires us all to create happy, healthy, humane places for people to work and live!

In 2019, Deri was nominated for induction into the Canadian Speaking Hall of Fame, where excellence on the platform in the top criteria. She adds extra value to her clients with certification in emotional intelligence, psychometric assessment, and neuro-linguistic programming. She is presently completing Compassionate Inquiry training through Dr. Gabor Mate. In early 2022, she will add completion of the CEOLC (Contemplative End of Life Care) program through the Institute of Traditional Medicine.

Deri's client resources include three books, 'Wake Up To Your Habits', 'What's Your Story? You Decide', and now this one, that all provide a rich resource of strategies and tools to shift your emotions, adjust your thinking, and positively impact your results. The books have become progressively more vulnerable, as Deri shares intimate stories from her life with the hope that they will positively contribute to the lives of others.

Ali Howorth, BA, DiamondFishARt

Ali is a lifelong learner and explorer, including post-secondary education in Asian Studies, American Sign Language, and most recently in Creative Communications.

After graduating from the University of Manitoba with a degree in Linguistics and Psychology in the middle of a pandemic (and having to move back into Mom and Dad's house!!), Ali decided to change directions and finally pursue their creative passion! They started DiamondFishArt on Instagram in August of 2020 as a way to practice and experiment with all kinds of creative and crafty mediums.

Ali finds much of their inspiration from Anime, Lord of the Rings, Harry Potter, and K-pop. Ali also doesn't hold back when it comes to bright colour; honestly, the brighter the better! As a part of the 2SLGBTQ++

community, Ali values and always attempts to go a bit against the mainstream in terms of their hair, clothing and makeup experimentation. They are a 'figure it out' kind of person, if they don't know how do something they will never let that slow them down, trial and error is a wonderful way of learning!

A big thank you has to go to the sweet pup, Bella, as she has kept Ali sane throughout the last eight years and her calming presence was a huge help in the design and creation of these illustrations.

Follow Ali's Art:

Instagram: https://www.instagram.com/diamondfishart/

YouTube: https://m.youtube.com/channel/UCMd18WjZTL5wm7WH7RxnM5A

TikTok: TikTok.com/@diamondfishart

Etsy: https://etsy.me/2Lij1iF

LET'S STAY CONNECTED!

Reach out and connect:

Website: DeriLatimer.com https://www.derilatimer.com/

Facebook: Deri Latimer https://www.facebook.com/deri.latimer

Linkedin: Deri Latimer https://ca.linkedin.com/in/derilatimer

Twitter: @derilatimer https://twitter.com/derilatimer?lang=en

Instagram: Deri Latimer https://www.instagram.com/
derilatimer/?hl=en

Youtube: Deri Latimer http://www.youtube.com/channel/
derilatimer

Email: deri@derilatimer.com

Deri would love to work with you! Her most popular Keynotes are:

Not Crazy, Just Human: How Learning to Feel Can Hurt … and Heal

Your Brain 'At Work': What Neuroscience Is Teaching Us About How to Live And Work Well

The Resilient Mindset: Practical Strategies for Growing Personal Resilience

A sampling of participant comments include:

"Her enthusiasm is contagious." – Best Buy Canada Ltd.

"That was amazing!" – Canadian Armed Forces

"You changed people." – Jim Pattison Group

"Please bring her back!"

– Great West Life Assurance Company of Canada

"Brain-energizing!" – Prairie South School Division

"You created a 'buzz'!"

– Canadian Association of Volunteer Resources

"We noticed immediate changes in our staff."

– National Leasing Inc.

Available at
derilatimer.com/store

Books

What's Your Story?

Wake Up to Your Habits

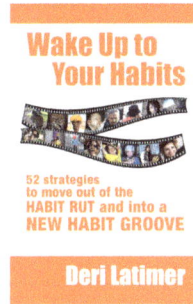

Desktop Strategy Cards

Recognition/Appreciation Cards

High Five

Show of Hands

Gratitude

.

www.ingramcontent.com/pod-product-compliance
Lightning Source LLC
Chambersburg PA
CBHW050841270326
41930CB00019B/3428